Fly-Fishing Techniques FOR Smallmouth Bass

Harry Murray

FLY-FISHING
TECHNIQUES
FOR Smallmouth
Bass
Harry Murray

Frank
Amato
PORTLAND

Dedication

This book is dedicated to my children: Milly, Nicki, Liz, Jeff and Susan

Acknowledgments

I am deeply indebted to many people who have helped tremendously in the preparation of this book. Without their assistance it could not have been written. Alphabetically, they are: Barry Beck, William Burslem, John Coleman, William Downey, Lefty Kreh, Jack McAllister, Jeff Murray, Cindy Simmons, Rob Simpson, Rhonda Tamkin, Charley Waterman, and Dave Whitlock

Other Books By The Author

Trout Stream Fly Fishing
Trout Fishing In The Shenandoah National Park
Fly Fishing For Smallmouth Bass
His Blessing Through Angling
Virginia Blue Ribbon Streams
Mastering The Mountain Trout Streams (video)
Fly Fishing For Smallmouth Bass (video)
Fly Fishing For Trout (DVD)

All inquiries should be addressed to:

Frank Amato Publications, Inc.
P.O. Box 82112, Portland, Oregon 97282
503•653•8108 • www.amatobooks.com

All photographs by Harry and Jeff Murray unless otherwise noted.
Tying illustrations by Dürten Kampmann
Book & Cover Design: Kathy Johnson
Printed in Singapore

Softbound ISBN: 1-57188-360-6 UPC: 0-81127-00194-1
Hardbound ISBN: 1-57188-362-2 UPC: 0-81127-00196-5

1 3 5 7 9 10 8 6 4 2

Contents

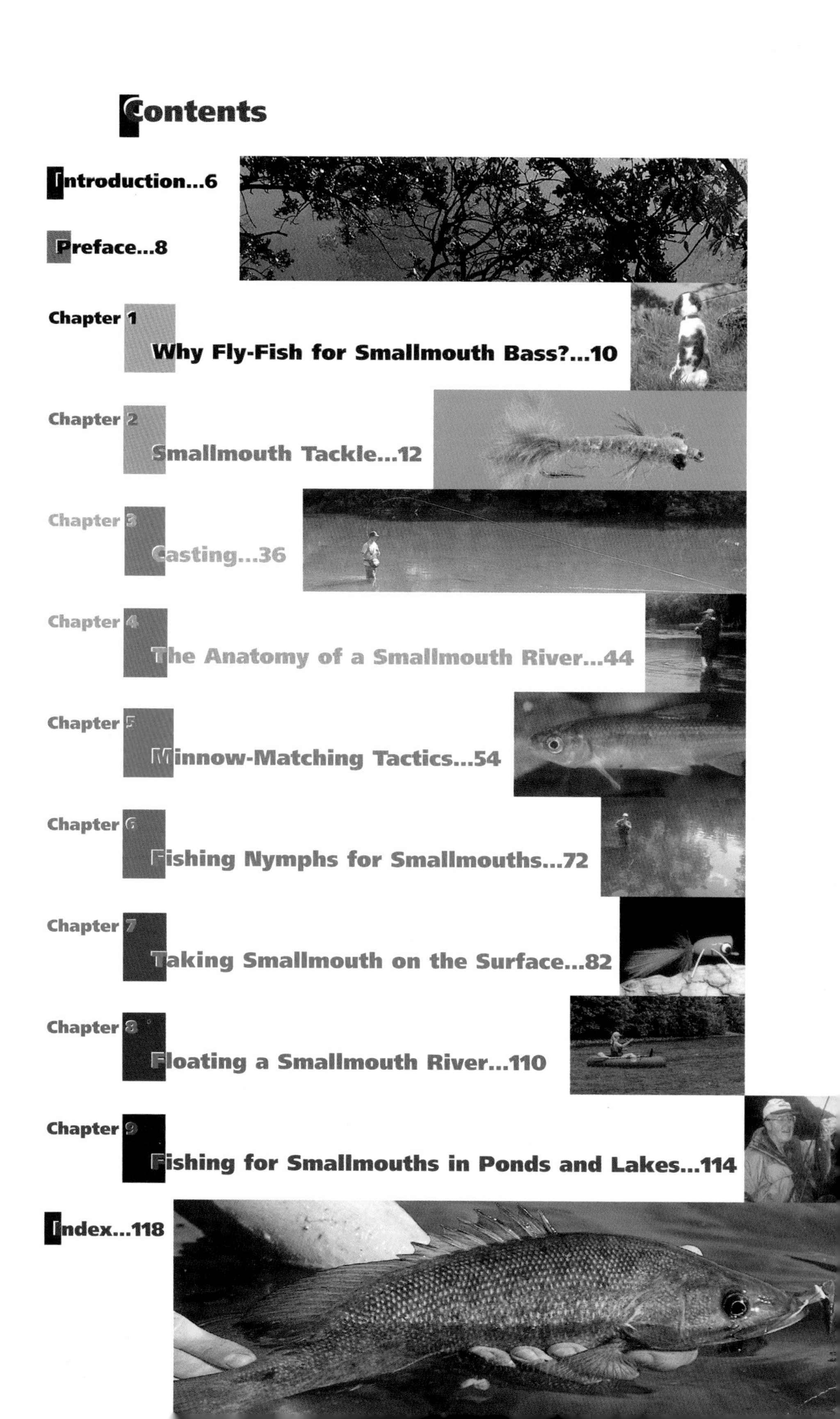

Introduction

A warm morning sun filled Montana's Paradise Valley as we worked our way along the banks of Armstrong Spring Creek. Pale morning duns were just beginning to show as the first trout of the morning confidently sipped in Cathy's imitation. In a rush the hooked trout tangled in the weeds and the angler and fish parted company. It often goes that way on this weed-choked spring creek. As Cathy started to reattach a new fly, another angler quietly appeared on the bank.

We both turned to say good morning when we heard, "Hi, I'm Harry." I remembered thinking Harry who? Well, sometimes you find yourself immediately liking someone just by their expression, and Harry's big smile quickly put us at ease. By the end of our short conversation we knew Harry Murray. That was many seasons ago and Harry has become a trusted and valued friend. We're thankful for this opportunity to share our thoughts on both the author and his new book.

The smallmouth bass may be Harry's first love. His passion and energy for the species comes through loud and clear in the text. This is a book that takes you through the ABC's of fishing for smallmouth and in typical Harry Murray fashion it's easy to read and understand. Although the main character is the smallmouth, the tactics and advice that Harry offers would benefit any freshwater fly-fisherman. Harry is a natural and gifted teacher and has that wonderful ability to get his message across without complications. But more than anything Harry loves to share his knowledge and enthusiasm of fly-fishing with anyone who will listen. That's what Harry is really about.

If you have never fished for smallmouth then you are missing out on one of the most sporting freshwater fish that you can catch on a fly. I remember a time when I was guiding a client on the lower end of our home stream Fishing Creek. We were fishing streamers and looking for a big trout. There was a hard stride and a hook-up followed by an unbelievable struggle with this yet unseen fish. Finally as the fish came to the net I heard the gasp when my angler realized he had a 20-inch smallmouth bass. He remarked later that he thought he had hooked the trophy brown of the pool and had no idea of how hard a smallmouth bass would fight.

Read Harry Murray's book, follow his instructions and you too could hook-up with that trophy of the pool.

—Barry Beck

Smallmouth rivers often flow through some of the most beautiful parts of our country, giving one extra gratification in just being there.

Preface

The smallmouth bass is a wonderful fish that holds different challenges for different anglers.

Some prefer to fish for them in the shaded coves of large lakes from fine large boats, while others enjoy floating large remote rivers with a canoe to lure them from beautiful grassbeds. The versatile personal kick boat enables one to slip away to sections of rivers that see few anglers and possibly some bass that are easy to fool.

However, the trend I see now is that many fly-fishermen enjoy going out on their own to wade the streams. These may be rivers that are several hundred yards wide that they drive days to reach, or a small creek behind their homes they fish in the evenings after work.

Likewise, different anglers take different approaches in the tactics they use. Some began taking smallmouths when they were youngsters fishing with a discarded broom handle, old black nylon line and using worms as bait. Later they might have progressed up to a crude casting outfit and live minnows as bait. Then they graduated to a smoother casting reel and more delicate rod, using plugs to lure their bass. Eventually they tried a fly rod.

At this point the route the individual takes depends on what he enjoys in angling. Some derive great joy from catching their bass on standard surface bugs and basic streamers and see no reason to complicate the game. Others, however, find great joy and gratification in delving deeper. They strive to understand the various foods in different parts of the rivers, how the bass feed upon them and even develop new flies and bugs that will enable them to catch more bass. The extent to which one desires to delve into the complexities of smallmouth angling is strictly a matter of personal preference, but the final goal is to have fun while angling.

The natural trend most smallmouth anglers take is that first they want to catch many fish each time they go. Next they become big-fish hunters seeking to catch the largest fish they can find. Finally, they strive to match their wits against the most challenging bass under the most demanding conditions. The last plateau that many anglers enjoy is the close contact they experience with their Creator as they stand alone in a beautiful river at sunset in the midst of His creation.

—Harry W. Murray

The author enjoys stalking the wary smallmouth bass late in the summer when the rivers are low and clear because of the challenge they afford.

Chapter 1

Why Fly-Fish For Smallmouth Bass?

I believe the smallmouth bass is the gentleman of the warmwater species. They take on the best traits of some of the finest game fish and blend them in a graceful bronze body that they proudly display by leaping into the air when we hook them.

I've had them sip in dry flies along a grassbed just like a brown trout, chase a streamer beside a deadfall as a largemouth does and grab my nymphs in heavy runs just like a rainbow trout. Their willingness to take our flies makes them very special to many serious anglers.

The smallmouth bass is an exciting challenge for anglers of all levels because they adapt their feeding habits to the specific season and stream conditions requiring that one be observant in order to catch them.

The smallmouth is capable of meeting the demands of anglers of all skill levels. I've had groups of Boy Scouts catch many smallmouths in shallow riffles on streamers early in the summer when the conditions were ideal and the bass apparently were quite hungry. I've also watched an expert fly-angler use his most stealthy upstream approach to present a delicate dry damselfly on a long leader to catch a large bass he spotted feeding on the naturals in a low, clear river late in the summer.

The possibilities between these two extremes permit one to find the type of fishing he enjoys most. You may be satisfied with an easy pace and casual fishing to catch those bass that are cooperative. Or, you may enjoy studying the intimate traits of the smallmouth bass in order to refine your angling skills to successfully match your wits against the natural instincts of the bass under the most demanding conditions.

A great feature of this quest is that frequently one can fly-fish for smallmouths in beautiful streams in solitude that one seldom finds when fishing for other species. And, in many cases this fine action can be found close to home. In order to cash in on good trout fishing, or wrestle with some big stripers, or stalk bonefish on the flats, many anglers have to be willing to spend a fair amount of time and money to fulfill these dreams. Whereas, the smallmouth is distributed broadly enough across the country that one can fish for them on the evenings after work, or with just very little more planning.

In this same respect, the smallmouth can give great fly-fishing in many parts of the country when the trout streams become too low or too warm late in the summer to provide good fishing.

If you haven't fished much for smallmouths, but have done other forms of fly-fishing, you probably already have many of the skills necessary for catching them.

For example, if you've fished sculpin streamers on the Yellowstone River in Montana or the Beaverkill River in New York, this same tactic works extremely well on smallmouths. Likewise, if you've drifted a big Dave's Hopper along the high banks of the Madison River above Ennis, Montana you already know how to take big smallmouths on drys during the summer. If you have spent time casting deer-hair bugs around grass islands for largemouth bass you already know one of my favorite ploys for fishing for river smallmouths late in the summer. If you've excitedly chucked big streamers on a nine-weight rod in front of stripers chasing bait through the salt water, you will find that this same tactic can give you some of the most exciting smallmouth fishing at dusk that any angler could want.

In order to help you broaden your angling skills so you can successfully fish for smallmouth under all of the conditions we encounter throughout the season, we'll incorporate some of these tactics you already know with some slightly different techniques that help meet their whims under various demanding conditions.

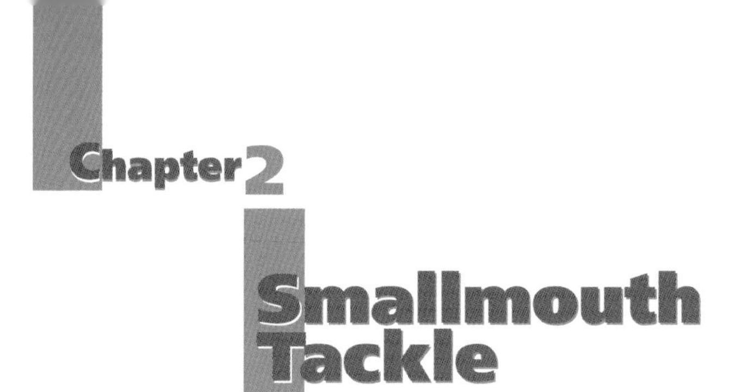

Chapter 2 Smallmouth Tackle

To gain the greatest amount of pleasure from their time on the wate,r most smallmouth anglers select tackle that's fine-tuned for this fishing. Some of this overlaps with tackle used for other types of fly-fishing, while other items are used more specifically for smallmouths.

Fly Rod

The fly rods favored by most serious smallmouth fly-fishermen are nine feet long that balance with number seven- or eight-weight lines. I use a seven-weight rod for

Fly-fishing for smallmouth bass is one of the most enjoyable forms of angling and is productive from early in the spring until later in the fall.

most of this fishing because it's a little lighter than a rod with comparable action that casts an eight-weight line, and the seven will handle the size flies I use most of the time. Only if I plan to fish mostly with size 4 and larger flies do I go to my eight-weight rod.

I prefer a fly rod that has a strong tip and a medium-action butt section. The strong tip makes it easy to pick up our bulky surface bugs and heavy underwater flies from the stream on the back cast. The medium action in the butt of the rod blends well with the wind-resistant nature of our bugs giving us a smooth, pleasant casting cycle. Rods built in this manner enable us to make very accurate casts and they are not tiring to use when fishing all day.

These rods come in both two-piece and multi-piece models. The major appeal of the multi-piece rods is their convenience when traveling. When traveling on airplanes, small cars, bikes or on horseback, a multi-piece rod is much easier to carry than a two-piece rod. Some multi-piece rods are a little more expensive than the two-piece models and, admittedly, the extra ferrules are just one more thing to break. Unless you find the shorter sections a great convenience you will probably be better off with the two-piece model.

Most fly rods are not broken while fishing but are broken around cars or by accidents at home. I always carry my rod in its case until I get to the stream. Then I put my waders and vest on and get everything ready, the last thing I do is get the rod out of the case. Then when I've finished fishing the first thing I do when I get back to the car is put my rod in its case. At home I take it out of the case and set it in the corner to dry overnight then I put it back in the case to protect it.

I use a good ferrule dressing on the rod ferrules about every fifth time I go fishing. This assures a smooth fit and prolongs the life of the ferrule.

Reels

Reels for smallmouth fly-fishing should be durable and have the capacity to hold the line and one hundred feet of backing. I like to have an extra spool for my reel and put my floating line on the reel and my sink-tip line on the extra spool. Large-arbor reels are popular now because their larger diameter enables us to crank in line faster than we can with a regular reel. This is a nice feature, but I prefer regular fly reels because they are very durable. Multiplying reels also give a greater rate of line recovery, but they are not popular now because of their extra weight.

I like to clean and oil my reels several times during a season of normal fishing. If I happen to get sand or grit in my reel I wash it thoroughly in the stream at the time and then when I get home I clean it out with a soft cloth and oil it. Some reels have drag mechanisms that are factory sealed and the manufacturers do not recommend oiling these so check the directions that comc with your reel.

Fly Line

The most important fly line for the smallmouth angler is a weight-forward bass-bug tapered floating line. These usually have shorter front tapers and more compacted heads than regular lines. In addition to smoothly casting our big surface bugs they are great for nymph fishing because it's easy to pick up a short line and quickly load the rod and cast the nymph back out without false casting.

My second line is a sink-tip line that has ten to fifteen feet of sinking line incorporated into the front portion of the line. I like one that sinks at about 2.5 to 4.25 inches per second. By putting this on the second spool for my reel I can easily switch back and forth from my floating line to my sink-tip line as the stream conditions dictate. I may switch to my sink-tip line in a very fast run or a deep pool anytime throughout the season. However, the two times I use my sink-tip lines most are in the spring when the streams are high and late in the fall when the cool streams prompt the smallmouths to locate in the deepest water.

Most rods handle one specific line size best so you should select the line which is specified on the butt section of the rod right above the grip. Since we are discussing bass rods these would be either seven- or eight-weight lines and would be labeled as WF-7-F BBT or WF-8-F BBT for the floating bass-bug tapered lines and WF-7-F/S or WF-8-F/S for the sink-tip lines with the appropriate sinking rate.

Backing

The most popular backing used for smallmouth fishing is twenty-pound Dacron.

This should be changed every three to four years and should be checked and retied to the fly line once a year. This is an excellent line that does not deteriorate quickly, but if it gets wet every time you go fishing it is wise to set your reel out where it can dry out when you get home, otherwise the whole thing gradually takes on the unpleasant odor of mildew.

Leaders

Leaders are very important in smallmouth fishing. In my schools leaders give the students more problems than any other piece of equipment. I prefer compound knotted tapered leader nine feet long tapered down to 2X or 3X for most of my smallmouth fishing with a floating line. To aid in detecting the basses' strikes I construct mine with five feet of fluorescent red Amnesia (TM) mono in the two butt sections. Onto this leader I install two tube-type Scientific Anglers indicators in the butt sections. The bright butt of the leader and the indicators are a great help in detecting strikes on underwater flies.

I do not believe the bright color in the upper sections of these leaders scare the fish and each year I sell thousands of these Bright Butt (TM) leaders in my fly shop.

Smallmouth bass, the gentlemen of the warm water, are a great challenge for the fly angler because they will take drys, nymphs and streamers in all types of water.

If, however, you are concerned about this you can easily construct your leaders with clear mono using the following formulas.

For sink-tip fly lines I like to use five-foot leaders tapered down to 2X or 3X because these enable us to fish our flies deeper than we can with a longer leader.

Here is a simple system I've been using for many years which helps in fishing smallmouth flies deeply if you don't want to invest in a sink-tip line. I call these "mini-sinking heads". Today there are many similar products on the market under a variety of names so let me explain the ones I've found helpful in smallmouth fishing.

I start by using sections of lead-core trolling line—or the fastest-sinking old fly line you can find. I cut these in various lengths from six inches up to forty-eight inches. I form a loop on each end of each section by folding it over about an inch and whipping a knot on it with fly-tying thread, then I coat this knot with Pliobond cement.

By incorporating one of these mini-sinking heads into about the middle of my nine-foot leader with a loop-to-loop connection I can fish my flies quite deeply. These are easy to install while fishing, taking only about a minute, and you don't even have to remove the fly. These do not cast as well as a sink-tip line, and are not as versatile, but they are much more economical. See the sketch on page 20 for how I place this in my leader.

Tippet

The tippet of a leader is that section to which the fly is attached. When you purchase a leader or tie your own with the following formulas the tippet is already on the leader. You never add a new tippet to a new leader unless you cut the existing tippet on it back to about eight inches to add a finer tippet.

For example, if you have a new 9-foot 2X leader and add 2 feet of 2X tippet to this, you will not be able to present flies smoothly because your tippet is now twice as long as it should be. Throughout the day as you change flies you shorten the tippet. When it gets back to 16 to 18 inches, cut the tippet off behind the knot and add a new tippet which is two feet long.

The diameter of the tippet which we express as X (ie., 2X, 3X) should be selected to balance with the size fly you are fishing. A larger fly needs a larger tippet to prevent the fly from twisting the tippet thus forming a weak tippet. A smaller fly permits us to use a smaller tippet which allows a more delicate presentation and a more natural drift of the fly.

Since we always know the size fly we plan to use, here is a formula to easily determine your correct tippet size. Fly size divided by 3 (constant) equals tippet in X. Example: Size 6 fly divided by 3 equals 2X tippet.

Leader Formulas

Murray's Bright Butt Leader Formulas (TM) 9 Foot					
9ft., 0X leader		9ft., 1X leader		9ft., 2X leader	
Diameter	Length	Diameter	Length	Diameter	Length
Red 25# Amnesia	42	Red 25# Amnesia	36	Red 25# Amnesia	36
Red 20# Amnesia	24	Red 20# Amnesia	24	Red 20# Amnesia	24
Umpqua .015	12	Umpqua .015	12	Umpqua .015	12
Umpqua .013	6	Umpqua .013	6	Umpqua .013	6
Umpqua .011	24	Umpqua .011	6	Umpqua .011	6
		Umpqua .010	24	Umpqua .009	24

	9ft., 3X leader		9ft., 4X leader	
	Diameter	Length	Diameter	Length
	Red 25# Amnesia	36	Red 25# Amnesia	36
	Red 20# Amnesia	24	Red 20# Amnesia	24
	Umpqua .015	6	Umpqua .015	6
	Umpqua .013	6	Umpqua .013	6
	Umpqua .011	6	Umpqua .011	6
	Umpqua .009	6	Umpqua .009	6
	Umpqua .008	24	Umpqua .007	24

It is very exciting to know where a specific, very large, smallmouth bass feeds and then try to catch it—especially when you have a cheering section.

Murray's Classic Leader Formulas (TM) 9 Foot

9ft., 0X leader		9ft., 1X leader		9ft., 2X leader	
Diameter	Length	Diameter	Length	Diameter	Length
.022	36	.022	36	022	36
.020	24	.020	18	.020	18
.017	12	.017	12	.017	12
.015	6	.015	6	.015	6
.013	6	.013	6	.013	6
.011	24	.011	6	.011	6
		.010	24	.009	24

Murray's Classic Leader Formulas (TM) 7 1/2 Foot

7 1/2 ft., 0X leader		7 1/2 ft., 1X leader		7 1/2 ft., 2X leader	
Diameter	Length	Diameter	Length	Diameter	Length
.022	36	.022	24	.022	24
.020	12	.020	18	.020	18
.017	6	.017	6	.017	6
.015	6	.015	6	.015	6
.013	6	.013	6	.013	6
.011	24	.011	6	.011	6
		.010	24	.009	24

(Maxima in two butt sections, Umpqua other sections)			
9ft., 3X leader		9ft., 4X leader	
Diameter	Length	Diameter	Length
.022	30	.022	30
.020	18	.020	18
.017	12	.017	12
.015	6	.015	6
.013	6	.013	6
.011	6	.011	6
.009	6	.009	6
.008	24	.007	24

(Maxima in two butt sections, Umpqua other sections)			
7 1/2 ft., 3X leader		7 1/2 ft., 4X leader	
Diameter	Length	Diameter	Length
.022	24	.022	24
.020	12	.020	12
.017	6	.017	6
.015	6	.015	6
.013	6	.013	6
.011	6	.011	6
.009	6	.009	6
.008	24	.007	24

Leader Tippet Comparing X Code and Diameter

Leader Tippet (Thousandths of an inch)	X Code	Pound Test (Approximate)
.003	8X	1
.004	7X	2
.005	6X	3
.006	5X	4
.007	4X	6
.008	3X	8
.009	2X	10
.010	1X	12
.011	0X	14

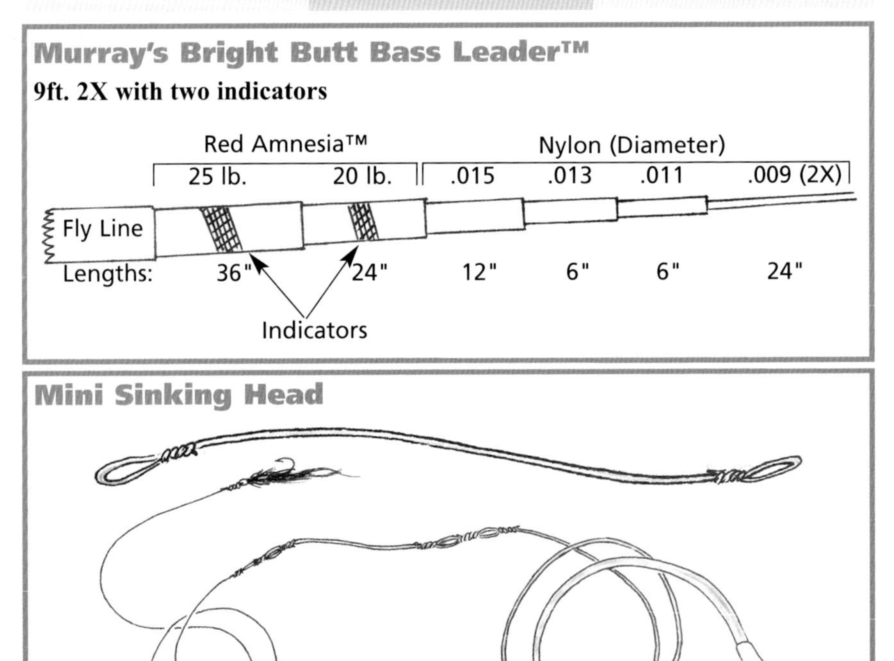

Knots

The smallmouth angler has a vast assortment of good knots from which to choose. The following knots are the ones most anglers rely upon to completely assemble their outfits from putting the backing on the reel to attaching the fly to the tippet.

Many of the large smallmouths we hook are lost because either the tippet knot or the fly-attaching knot breaks. In order to land more of these bass I encourage practicing tying these knots until you become proficient with them and then test them frequently while you're fishing; while you are fishing every fifteen to twenty minutes grasp the fly in one hand and the leader above the tippet knot in the other and pull firmly. If the knots are still secure you are in good shape, but if either one breaks simply tie it again. Admittedly this takes a few minutes but it is much better than losing the best bass of the season because a weak knot breaks.

Tying Backing to the Reel

I tie an overhand knot in the end of 20-pound-test Dacron backing line and attach this to the reel spool with an arbor knot. This is basically a slip knot which slides down tightly against the reel arbor. Wind on enough backing to fill about one half of the depth of the spool. Be careful not to add so much backing that the fly line will hit against the reel pillars. This will damage the finish of the fly line. Reel manufacturers give guidelines as to the amount of backing each reel will hold with different line sizes.

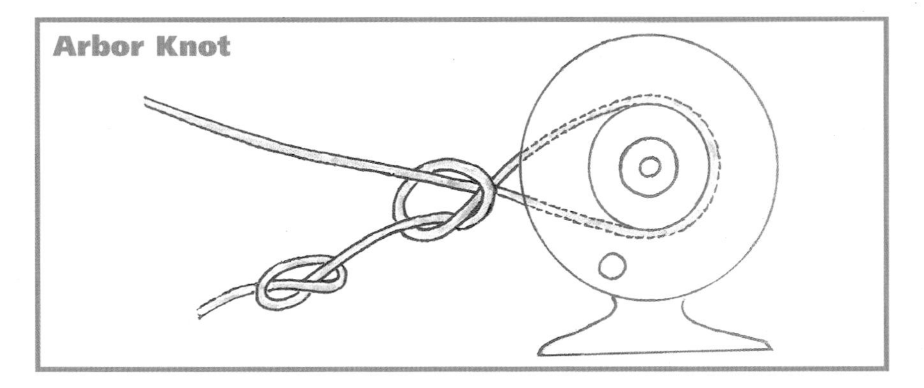

Albright Knot

Tying Fly Line to the Backing

The Albright knot is an excellent knot for attaching the fly line to the backing.

Pull about three feet of the end of the fly line marked "this end to reel" from its plastic spool. Form a loop in the end of the fly line by folding about two inches of the end of the line back over itself. While holding this loop in your left hand, insert about six inches of the backing through this loop, and while holding the backing under your left thumb, begin wrapping the backing toward the end of the loop in the fly line.

Make 10-12 wraps of the backing from left to right with each wrap snug against the previous wrap.

Insert the end of the backing through the loop in the end of the fly line opposite of where it entered originally so that both pieces of the backing come out beside each other.

With your left forefinger and thumb, slide the loops of backing to 1/8 inch from the end of the loop in the fly line. While holding the loops in place with your left forefinger and thumb, pull on the short tag end of the backing to firm up the wraps. Next pull the standing (long) part of the backing, then finally pull both pieces of backing. Trim off the tag end of the fly line and backing

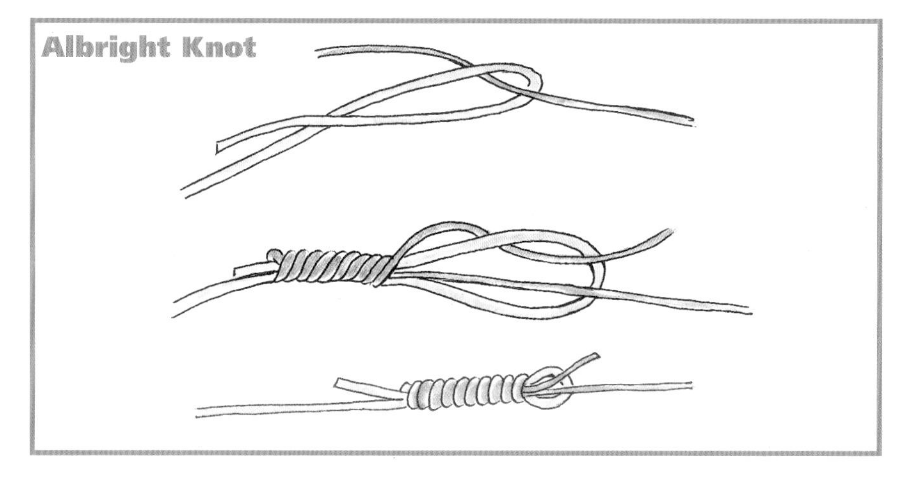

Nail Knot and Tube Knot

Attaching Leader to the Fly Line

After you wind all of the fly line onto the reel, except the last three feet, you are ready to attach the leader to the line.

1. Nail Knot or Tube Knot

The easiest knot to use for this is a nail knot or tube knot.

Hold the end of the fly line and the tube between the thumb and forefinger of your left hand with about two inches of the tube and the fly line sticking out to the right. Form a ten-inch loop in the butt of the leader with your right hand. With your left hand hold this loop tight against the tube. Use your right hand to hold the short end of the leader and make five tight wraps to the right over the tube and the fly line so these wraps are tight against each other about 1/2 inch from the end of the fly line.

While holding the wraps in place with your left-hand thumb and forefinger, use your right hand to insert the end of the leader through the tube from right to left. Slide the tube out, and while keeping the wraps in place with your thumbnails, tighten them by pulling the leader on both sides of the knot. Next pull the fly line and leader to lock the knot in place.

Clip off the tag end of the leader and fly line.

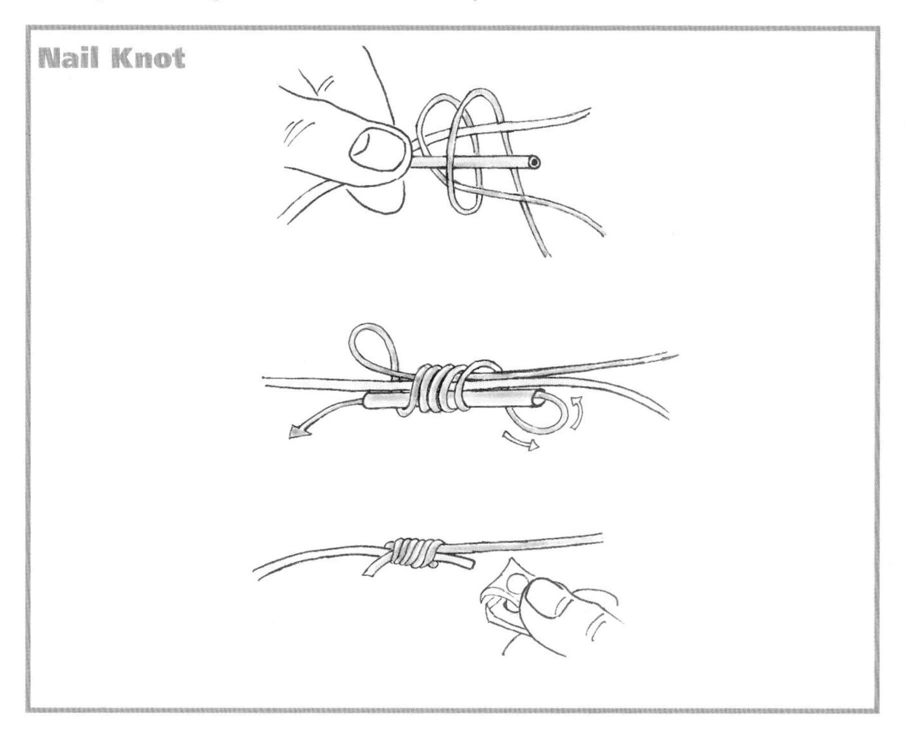

2. Needle Knot

This is an alternate knot for attaching the leader to the fly line. It is similar to the nail knot except the butt of the leader is inserted into the center of the fly line giving a smoother connection.

Shave down about two inches of the butt of the leader with a razor blade to a fine point. Insert a small-diameter needle into the center of the end of the fly line and punch this out of the side of the fly line about 1/4 inch up. Stick the butt of the leader into the eye of the needle and pull this through the fly line so it extends out about six inches.

Place the end of the fly line tight against the needle with the end of the line even with the eye of the needle. Make four tight, snug wraps with the butt of the leader over the line and needle from left to right. Insert the end of the leader into the eye of the needle and pull the needle out to the left being careful to retain the four wraps.

Use your thumbnails to hold the wraps together and slide them toward the point where the leader sticks out of the side of the fly line. Pull on the leader on both sides of the wraps to lock the knot into place. Trim off the tag end of the leader and the knot is complete. You can coat this with several thin coats of Pliobond or Flexament if you want to make it very smooth.

Needle Knot

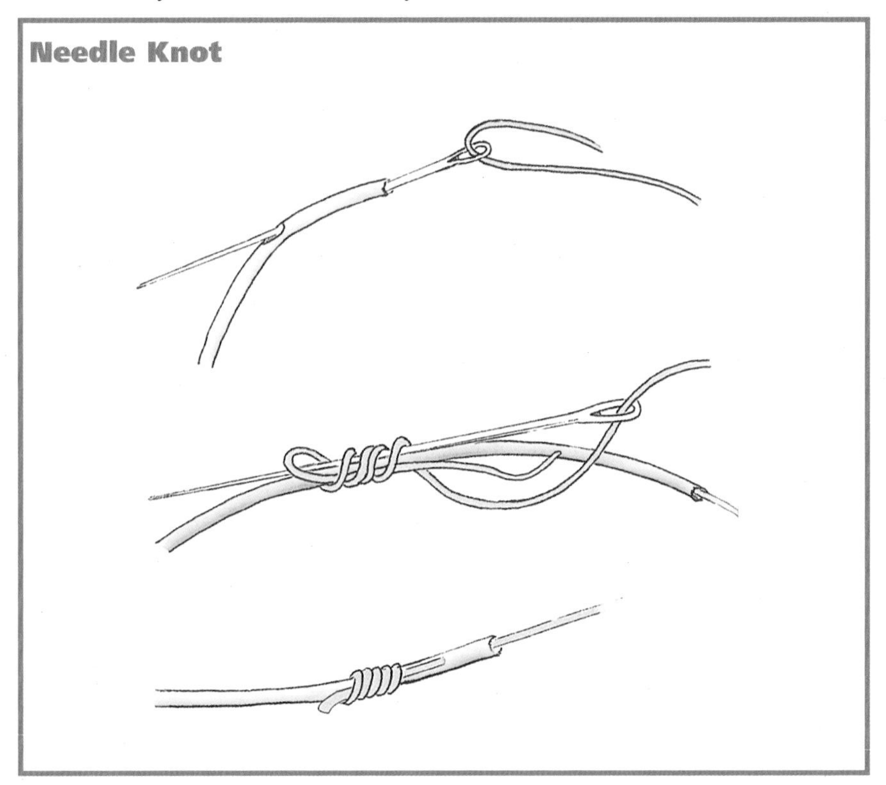

Surgeon's Knot

Tying the Tippet to the Leader

The surgeon's knot is a strong knot used to attach the tippet to the leader and it is easy to tie even in low-light levels.

Clip three feet of tippet material from the spool. Allow about five inches of this to lie beside the end of the leader. Form a loop and tie a simple overhand knot, being sure to pull the whole tippet through the loop, along with the end of the leader.

While retaining the open loop with the thumb and forefinger of your left hand, insert the tippet and the end of the leader through the loop the second time.

Pull both pieces of mono on each side of the knot until it draws down tightly, then clip off the two short ends.

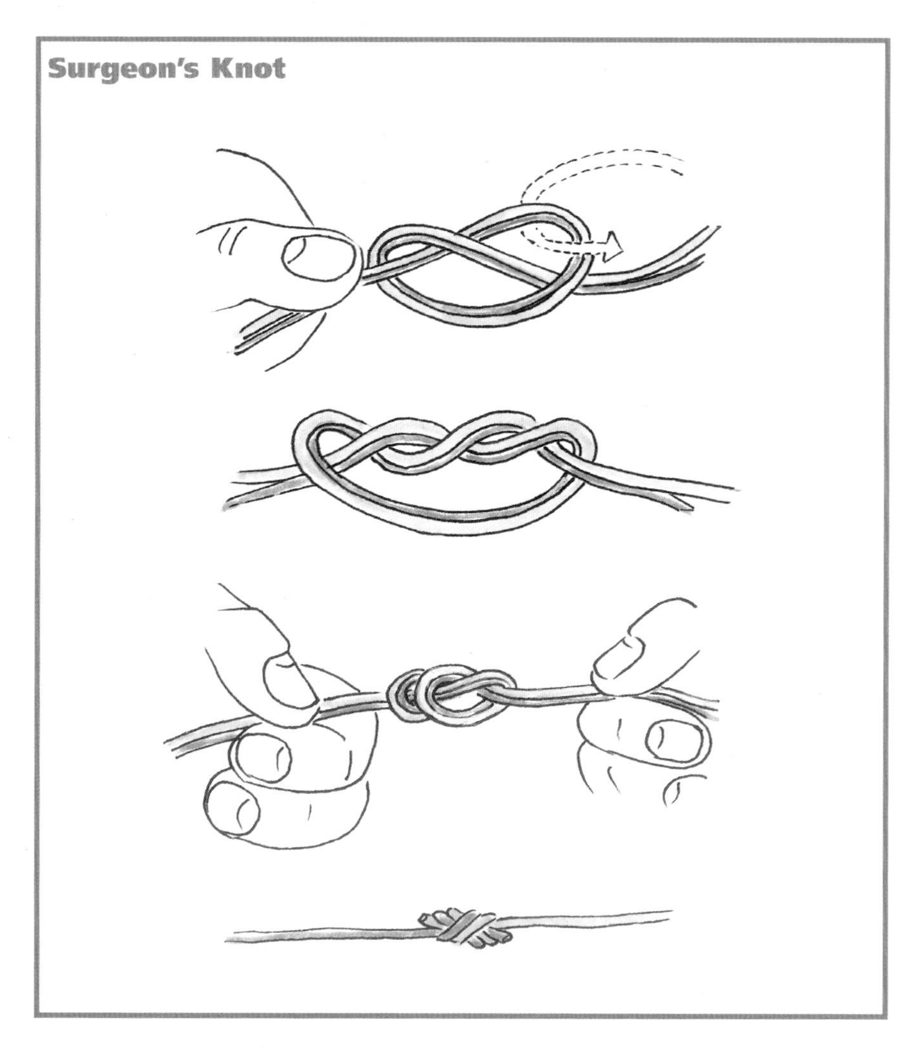

Improved Clinch Knot

Tying the Fly to the Tippet

The improved clinch knot is a good knot for tying the fly onto the tippet.

Insert about five inches of the tippet through the eye of the fly. Make five wraps of the tag end of the tippet around the standing part of the tippet while holding the fly firmly. Insert the tag end of the tippet through the gap formed immediately in front of the eye of the fly. Pull five inches through this gap, then insert it in the loop over the wraps, and pull gently on the standing part of the tippet.

While holding the fly securely, pull firmly on the standing part of the leader until all of the wraps in the knot draw down tightly.

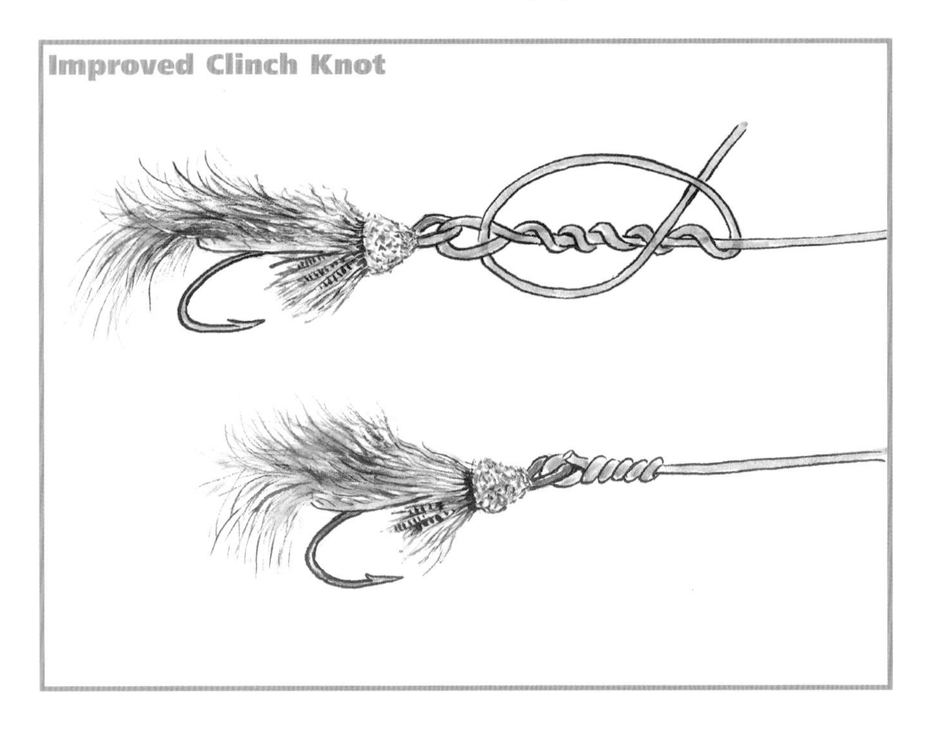
Improved Clinch Knot

Surgeon's Loop Knot

This is a very strong knot that is easy to tie, making it an excellent choice for the smallmouth angler in many places. I use this mid-leader when I'm inserting a mini-sinking head. If you like to change leaders frequently you can tie this on the leader butt and onto a six-inch piece of .022 inch mono attached to the fly line with a needle knot and thus change your leader in less than a minute with a loop-to-loop connection.

Surgeon's Loop Tying Steps

Step 1: Fold three inches of mono back over itself.

Step 2: Form a one-inch loop in the fold.

Step 3: Insert the folded tip through the one-inch loop and pull it out about one inch.

Step 4: Repeat Step 3.

Step 5: Pull on the loop and the standing part of the mono and the tag end of the mono all at the same time. I find that by inserting the end of my clippers or forceps into the loop it is easy to snug this knot tightly.

Step 6: Cut the tag end of the mono.

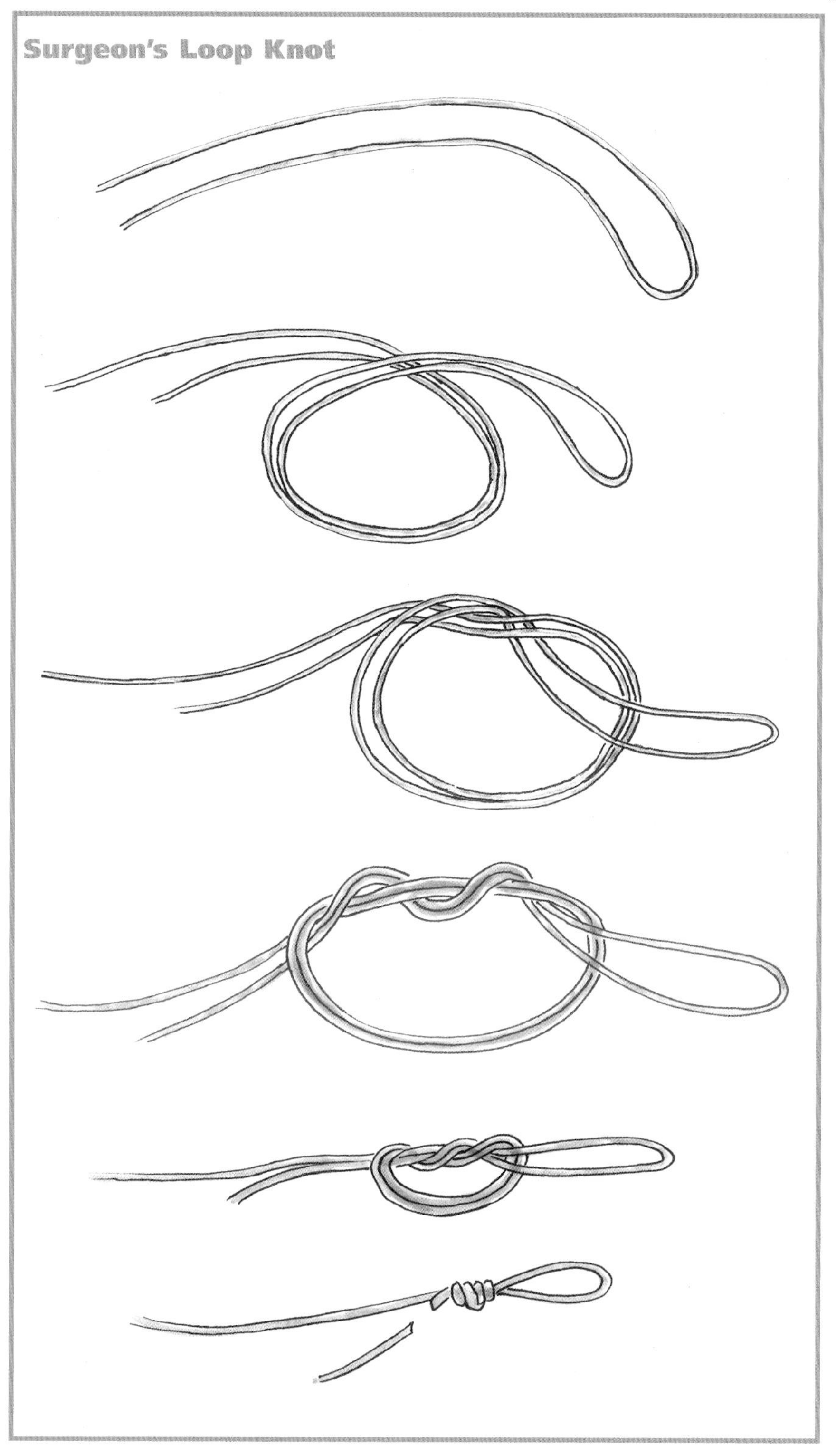
Surgeon's Loop Knot

Early fall is a great time to fish the rivers for smallmouth bass because they often go on a feeding frenzie, apparently building up their strength for the winter.

Waders

The smallmouth angler's wading gear should be determined by the temperature of the water he plans to fish.

If you plan to fish in the spring and fall, when the water is cool, you will want chest-high waders. I like those constructed of breathable waterproof material because they are light weight and very comfortable. Some waders are constructed with neoprene which is quite warm and some with coated nylon which is very economical. These can be purchased with a boot foot, which are complete as they are, or with a stocking foot which requires a separate wading shoe. I prefer the latter because during the summer when the water is warm I can leave the waders at home and wade wet with a pair of slacks and the wading shoes. This is much more comfortable than using chest-high waders and saves wear on the waders.

Felt-sole waders and shoes give better traction than rubber soles when wading and felts with tungsten carbide studs are even better.

Wading Staff

A sturdy wading staff that folds into short sections that fits into a holster attached to your wader belt is a great help when wading slippery or fast rivers. Be sure it is stout enough to support you if you slip and suddenly throw all of your weight onto it. I've gotten into trouble when flimsy wading staffs bent or telescoping staffs collapsed.

Vest

I like a smallmouth vest that is a little shorter than most trout vests because in warm weather when I'm wading wet I may get into very deep water and the shorter vest helps keep its contents dry. The mesh style is nice because it is light and cool in hot weather. I like several large pockets in the front because my bass fly boxes are large and I like a full-width large-bellows zippered pocket in the back which will hold my lunch, drinking water, raincoat and a small pouch of emergency items. The top-of-the-line vests that meet these guidelines are usually a good investment because they are more comfortable and more durable than budget vests.

Raincoats

The ideal raincoat for the smallmouth wading angler should be lightweight, waterproof, breathable, hooded, long enough to reach over the top of the waders, and large enough to comfortably fit over a loaded vest with the most bulky clothing you plan to wear.

If you plan to do most of your fishing from a boat or canoe and not use waders you may want a longer raincoat and rain pants.

Follow the manufacturers recommendations closely for the proper care of your raincoat in order to get the longest life and most comfortable use of it. Even the finest raincoats can "wet out" with improper care.

Hats

A good fishing hat or cap should stop or slow a moderate rain, keep the sun off your head and, with a dark underneath side of the brim, shade your eyes to aid in seeing through the water. In cold weather you may want the warmth that a wool or poly fleece hat can give. During the summer, a lightweight cap with vented mesh sides is nice. A waterproof breathable material is great, but you can spray non-waterproof caps with Tectron(TM) or a similar waterproofing treatment and get pretty good protection in modest rains.

Sunglasses

Sunglasses are one of the most important items a smallmouth angler owns. In fact, I carry a spare pair in my vest in case I lose the first pair on the stream. These should be polarized and I prefer the lightest tinted tan or yellow lens I can find. These glasses enable you to clearly see through the glare on the surface of the water so you can accurately evaluate the stream bottom in order to know where the bass will hold and feed. The glasses holders that go over the head are nice because if you fall, they may prevent you from losing your glasses.

Flashlight

Some of the best smallmouth fishing happens quite late in the evening. It is helpful to have a small flashlight for when you are changing flies, and to help you get safely back to the car in the dark.

Angling Tools

There are many little gadgets we use frequently on the streams that simplify our fishing. Here are the ones I use most:

- I like to attach a pair of small leader clippers to the front of my vest with a small retractor reel.
- My hook-sharpening file is also attached to the front of my vest with a retractor reel.
- Silicon cream to aid in floating dry flies and hair bugs can be attached to the vest with a small retractor reel or stored in a pocket.
- A leader straightener is a great help in taking the curl out of your leader when you begin fishing each day, you may need it several times during the day.
- Needlenose pliers are very useful for mashing down hook barbs and for making small repairs.
- Forceps are great for grasping the hook in order to gently release fish.
- Knot-tying tools are good if you are not comfortable in tying knots freehand.
- If I'm fishing in poisonous snake country I always carry a Sawyer Extractor (TM) snake-bite kit in the back of my vest.
- Stream thermometers are nice if you find it interesting to evaluate feeding activities at various water temperatures.

Emergency Bag

I carry a gallon-size ziplock plastic bag with assorted items for emergency use: a butane lighter, ferrule cement, wader-patching kit, duct tape, referee's whistle, Band-Aids, pencil stub, Swiss Army knife, rod tip top and snake guide and jar-opening grips to free stuck ferrules.

Smallmouth Flies and Bugs

Smallmouths often show a definite preference in the flies and bugs they will take. Here is a selection of patterns that have proven themselves by catching smallmouth bass all across the country.

Streamers

Silver Outcast

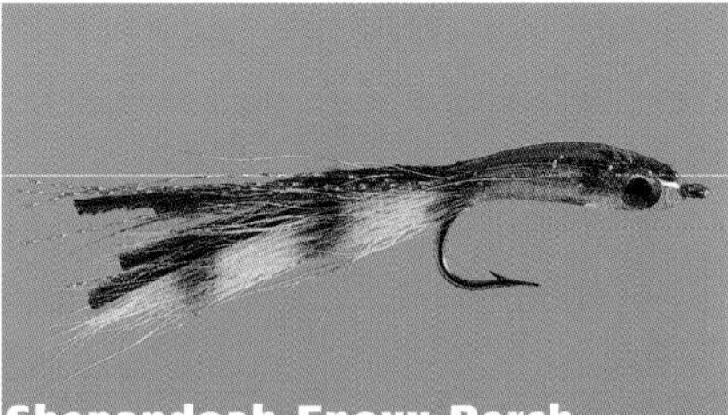
Shenandoah Epoxy Perch

Shenandoah Epoxy Shiner

Murray's Madtom/Sculpin

Whitlock's Hare Water Pup

Murray's Shiner

Murray's Chub

Murray's Sunfish

Clouser's Crawfish

Singer's Crawfish

Clouser's Deep Sculpin

Clouser's Deep Silver Shiner

Clouser's Deep Golden Shiner

Whitlock's Sculpin

Shenk's White Streamer

Shenk's Sculpin

Murray's Wounded Minnow

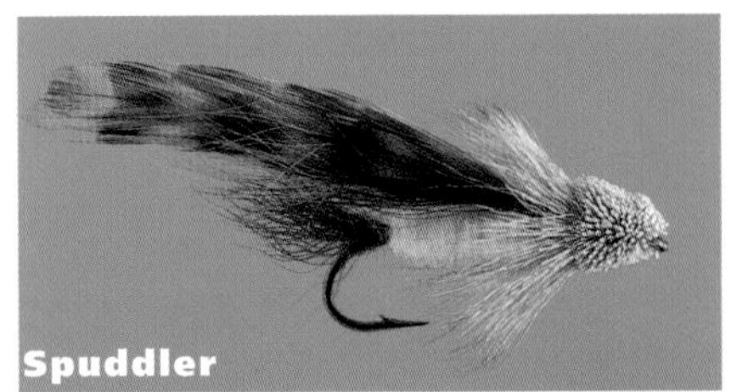
Spuddler

Mr. Rapidan Streamer

White Zonker

Black Woolly Bugger

Olive Woolly Bugger

White Marabou Muddler

Murray's Pearl Marauder

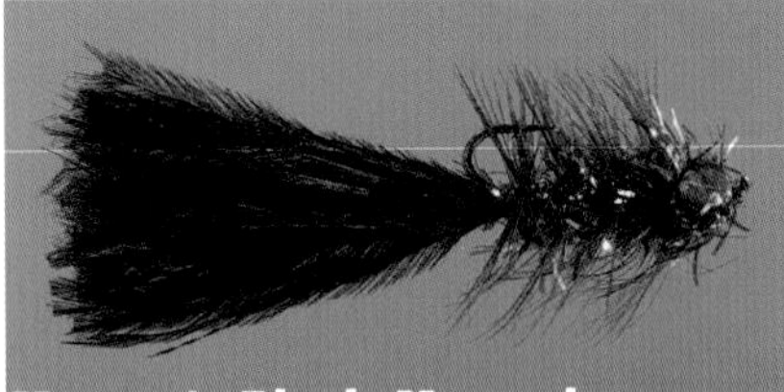
Murray's Black Marauder

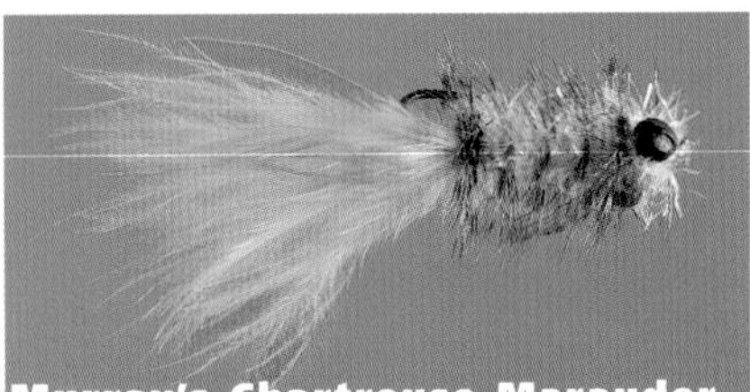
Murray's Chartreuse Marauder

James Wood Bucktail

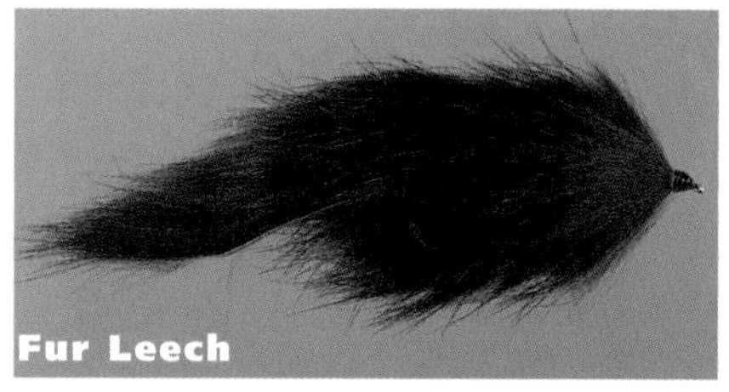
Fur Leech

Nymphs

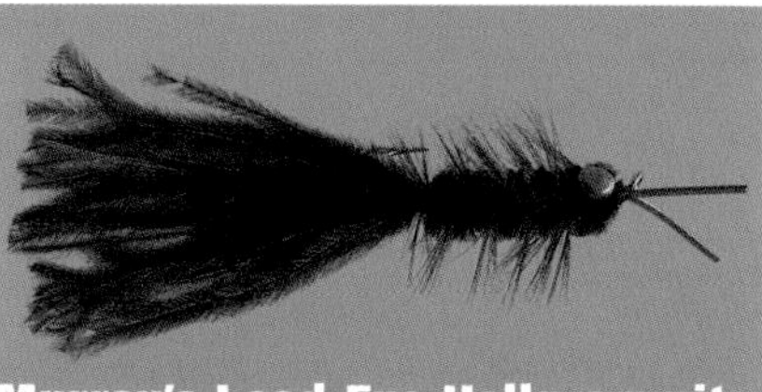
Murray's Lead Eye Hellgrammite

Bitch Creek Nymph

Casual Dress Nymph

Murray's Road Kill Nymph

Murray's Ghost Nymph

Whitlock's Red Squirrel Nymph

Dragonfly Nymph

Damselfly Nymph

Murray's Olive Strymph

Murray's Black Strymph

Murray's Cream Strymph

Bugs and Dry Flies

Murray's Shenandoah Blue Popper

Murray's Shenandoah Sunfish Slider

Murray's Shenandoah Chugger

Lefty's Potomac Popper

Tapply Dear Hair Bug, Green/White

Shenandoah Hair Popper, Yellow

Shenandoah Hair Popper, Black

Whitlock's Mouserat

Whitlock's Frog

Dahlberg Diving Bug, Frog

Dahlberg Diving Minnow, Silver

Mr. Rapidan Skater

Murray's Blue Damsel Skater

Irresistible Dry

Elk Hair Caddis

Murray's Bass Hopper

Shenk's Letort Hopper

Shenk's Cricket

Dave's Hopper

Light Humpy

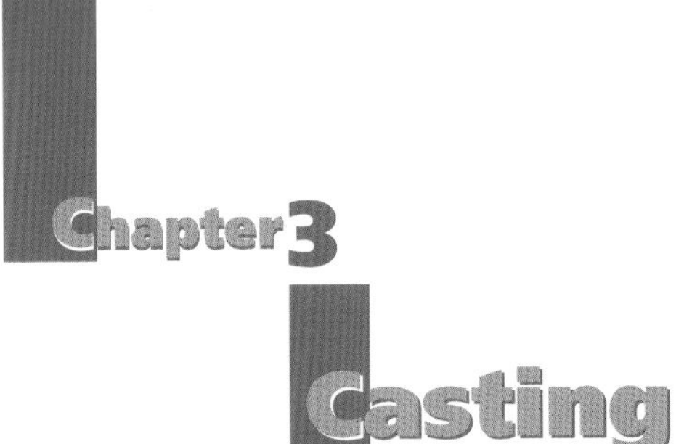

Chapter 3

Casting

Fly casting for smallmouth bass is basically the same as for other species. We seldom need the delicacy in presenting our flies that we use when presenting our small dry flies to trout in low, clear trout streams. However, there are a few situations where we can catch more bass and simplify our techniques by making some slight adaptations in our casting methods.

Accuracy in bug and fly placement can be extremely important in smallmouth fishing. For example, I've had many times when a large bass would not take a surface bug if it fell several feet short of the target I was shooting at, then take it solidly when it landed right beside the bass's feeding station. An inaccurately presented nymph or streamer may fail to drift into the pocket you suspected the bass would hold even if you read it properly to start with.

The white Miller hatch provides fast action at dusk when the emerging of the duns, the molting, mating, egg laying and spinner fall are all packed into about an hour. Careful planning will enable you to catch some large fish.

Since smallmouths do not like bright sunlight you may be able to improve your action greatly if you know a few tricks that will help you drift your bugs way back under some of the overhanging tree limbs along the banks.

Wind can cause a problem with all types of fly-fishing, but fortunately there are a few ways we can cope successfully with modest winds when fly-fishing for smallmouths.

Some of our nymphs and streamers are very heavy and although conventional casting techniques work there is an alternative that may make this easier for you.

Bulky surface bugs, especially the cupped-face Chuggers, can cause a great racket when we pick them off the water on the back cast and might scare any bass close by. To prevent this, I like to start the bug sliding along the surface with my line hand then smoothly pick it up with the rod.

Smallmouths have tough mouths and setting the hooks securely with large flies can be difficult at times. To help set the hook solidly and quickly the instant I get a strike I use a line-hand strike while also striking with a firm uplifting rod motion.

The Basic Cast

This is the starting point for all of the casts used in smallmouth fly-fishing. By understanding these principals and practicing them you can quickly develop a feeling for the proper timing and easily master all of the situations encountered while fishing.

The basic cast begins with the rod tip pointed straight down the fly line toward the water while holding the line firmly in the line hand.

With the wrist of your rod hand locked, begin to smoothly bring the fly rod up to about ten o'clock by simply lifting your forearm.

At this point, snap your wrist back firmly so the rod accelerates back to one o'clock, sending the fly line high into the air behind them. It is very important that one use enough power on the back cast to fully extend the line behind you. The best way to assure yourself that you are doing this properly is to actually look back over your shoulder and watch your line to be sure it's high and straight behind you.

With the fly line extended behind you, begin your forward cast by snapping your wrist forward and starting to move your forearm forward. As the fly line accelerates forward, continue pushing firmly with your forearm.

Follow through by turning the tip of the fly rod over so the cast will be delivered straight and accurate. If you find you need to make longer casts, you shoot the line forward by applying extra power as you push the rod forward and release the slack line from your line hand as the line accelerates forward.

The Roll Cast

The roll cast is excellent for several different purposes. If you have a high bank or tree limbs close behind you, this cast will enable you to easily present your cast out in front of you. When you have a ten to thirty feet of slack line on the water in front of you, the roll cast pick-up will help you get your fly out, where the conventional pick-up cast can come close to hitting you in the face. With deeply sunk flies on a sink-tip fly line, the roll cast pick-up will help you get these flies up close to the surface where you can make a regular cast.

With the fly line on the water in front of you, while holding the line firmly in your line hand, lift the fly rod to the two o'clock position over your shoulder. Stop here and allow the fly line on the water to come to a complete stop. Raise the fly rod by fully extending your rod arm and move it forward to the one o'clock position.

Begin your forward cast here by pushing the rod tip forcefully forward to the ten o'clock position. The fly line will be pulled from the water and will roll forward in front of you. After the loop of the fly line begins turning over in front of you, drop the rod tip to nine o'clock and the fly will be neatly delivered in front of you.

Casting Under Tree Limbs

Each year I take some of my best bass from beneath tree limbs hanging out over the rivers along the banks. I believe there are three good reasons for this: The shade here is definitely appealing to the large bass and they will often feed here all day long. Also there is an abundance of natural food here that falls into the river from the stream bank and overhanging limbs. Finally, some anglers pass these areas up because they don't like the hassle of hanging their flies and lures in the trees so you may be fishing to bass that get little angling pressure. Hopefully, this will make them easier to catch.

An easy way to cast under overhanging tree limbs is to face this area from about forty feet out in the river. After a regular back cast, drop the rod tip down to the side to where the rod is pointed just slightly above parallel to the water. Make a sidearm forward cast with enough force to send your bug back under the tree limbs. Be alert because often the bass take the bug in the first several seconds. When the wind is blowing strongly this same side arm cast will permit you to keep much of your fly line down close to the water where it is out of the way of some of the worst gusts.

Casting Heavily-Weighted Flies

There are certain conditions where you can catch some of the largest bass by using large, heavily -weighted nymphs and streamers. Admittedly these can be awkward to cast if you use the same method you use for casting a small trout fly, but a technique the late Charley Brooks showed me simplifies this. He called it "in low and out high."

With the fly deep in the water in front of you, pull in all of the slack with your line hand and extend the fly rod low out in front of you.

Use a low, sweeping, forceful side-arm motion to load the rod, then gradually sweep the rod up high behind you to send your back cast high.

When the rod loads behind you, begin a smooth overhead presentation cast with a gradually accelerating motion. This is a very accurate cast and it greatly reduces your chances of hitting yourself with the heavy flies.

Smooth Bug Pick-Up

There are many situations when it is necessary to pick a popper up from the surface to cast it to another spot close by. A noisy pick-up can easily scare any bass in

Point the rod tip down the line toward the spot where the fly line leaves the water. With the line hand, remove all of the slack line between the rod tip and the bug and begin to slowly slide the bug along the surface of the water.

Use a smooth uplifting rod motion while continuing to slide the bug along the surface with the line hand. The bug will come up off the water quietly and by using a regular back cast, the bug will sail smoothly up behind you.

the vicinity, so here is an easy method of getting the bug up off the water on your back cast.

Line-Hand Strike

Developing the habit of setting the hook firmly with the line hand, in addition to the rod, when the bass takes your fly or bug will give you many fish each season that you previously dismissed as "missed strikes". This is because you can quickly telegraph your hook-setting force to the bass. This is especially valuable when making long casts, or when the stream currents create curves in the fly line or when you are a little late in detecting the bass's take.

At the first hint of a take, impart a firm jerk with the line hand while simultaneously lifting the rod in a regular strike. This quickly telegraphs the strike to the bass assuring a high percentage of hooked fish.

In most cases you will want to use the line-hand strike in conjunction with the rod strike because of the efficiency of this method. However, a fringe benefit of developing a fast, firm line-hand strike comes late in summer when the rivers are low and the bass are wary.

If a bass comes to your surface bug in this low, clear water you can set the hook with just your line hand without causing a great disturbance. If it misses your bug, or you miss it, you can easily cast back to the same area and maybe catch him or another bass close by.

Chapter 4

The Anatomy of a Smallmouth River

Smallmouth bass have a great ability to adapt to many different types of cover throughout our rivers. Some locations are selected primarily as feeding stations because of the great amount of food they provide. Other locations are chosen as holding areas, or you might say homes, because of the security they offer. In some cases these qualities overlap and we find what I call a "primary feeding station." Loosely defined, I consider these as being those locations in the stream that hold the largest smallmouth in that part of the stream.

The smallmouth has also learned to adapt to all water levels, from the highest spring floods to the lowest summer drought. Not only have they learned to survive these two extremes, and everything in between, they know where to feed efficiently under all of these conditions.

In a lifetime of stalking the smallmouth, they have shown me that there are basically three factors that influence when, where and how they feed.

The heads of the pools are the natural habitat of great numbers of Hellgrammites. Fishing these areas, upstream, with a dead-drifting technique is very productive.

First and foremost, smallmouth do not like bright sunlight. They especially like to feed at dusk and dawn when the light is low. Heavily overcast, even drizzly days, are to their liking for the same reason. So how can we expect to catch worthy bass in the middle of a bluebird day? By concentrating on the natural shade the river affords the bass. Shaded banks, the shady side of an island, and the shade provided by boulders, ledges and grassbeds have all given me great fishing during the middle of a sunny day.

The second factor that governs the smallmouth's feeding habits is the natural availability of food. They have learned that there are many shiner minnows on the gravel bars, that the cobblestone tails of the pools are loaded with madtoms and that the riffles are the homes of great numbers of hellgrammites—and they have this knowledge of the *whole* river.

The third thing that influences their feeding mannerisms is the necessity to feed efficiently. Simply stated, they must derive more food value from every morsel they eat than the energy required to capture it. For example, they will not be found holding in the most powerful current in a riffle in order to feed on the hellgrammites that riffle holds, as they must have something to block the full force of the current from their bodies. This could be a boulder, a log, a grassbed or simply a depression in the stream bottom. Basically, they want to get as close to their food, or the current carrying it, as they possibly can while still maintaining protection from the current.

An effective way in which we can take advantage of these feeding habits of the smallmouth is to learn to read the various parts of the rivers. By this I mean learn to evaluate where the bass are expected to feed. Next you will see where to present your fly, and finally how to approach that specific area.

Using the following photographs we'll start in the upper reaches of a typical smallmouth river pool and fish the various portions of the pool all the way down to the tail of the pool.

Head of the Pool

The portion of the pool where the stream enters a pool from above is usually referred to as the head of the pool. I always devote extra time to fishing this area because it is usually very productive. Many large bass are attracted to the heads of the pools because of the great numbers of hellgrammites and sculpin minnows that make their homes here. The bass can easily hold securely around the boulders on the stream bottom and pick off an easy meal. When the rivers drop and become warm late in the summer, the extra oxygen pounded into the water in the riffles is apparently appealing to the bass because you can almost always pick up some good bass here, even late in the summer.

I like to fish the heads of the pools upstream with a Murray's Hellgrammite with an upstream dead-drifting technique. This method helps me drift my fly deeply when the river is carrying a great amount of water because I can easily negate the strong crossing currents. I find the upstream approach beneficial when the rivers get low late in the summer because I don't scare as many fish by wading upstream.

Head Riffle

The bass are often broadly distributed below the riffles entering the main part of the pool because there are great populations of nymphs and minnows throughout this area. If this area is less than three feet deep it usually holds mostly small bass during most of the day. However, large bass move into this area to feed at dusk and dawn.

The across-stream streamer technique is very effective here because it enables you to easily cover all of the water and it is easy to detect the strikes. I have very good success here with Shenk's Sculpin, Whitlock's Sculpin and Clouser's Sculpin.

Head Ledges

Head ledges are much like head riffles in that they feed the currents from above down into the main parts of the pools. The main difference is that there are often some four- to-five-foot-deep cuts in the stream bottom in the first five to twenty feet downstream of these ledges. This is one of those areas I was referring to as

Head-ledges are great for the bass because they provide food, cover and oxygen.

being both the homes and feeding stations for the bass. Thus you can expect to catch large bass here regularly.

The same across-stream streamer tactic used below the head riffles is very effective here. However, if the current is exceptionally fast you may find that going to a moderately fast sink-tip fly line (about 2.5 to 4.25 ips) will enable you to catch more bass because this will help you get your streamers deeper.

The Mid-Pool Area

The middle portion of the pools in many smallmouth rivers hold many bass because they can find good protection, and even shade, around the boulders and cuts along the stream bottom. During periods of low water these areas often attract bass from other areas because this is normally the deepest part of the pool. Apparently they feel safe here.

Dave Whitlock often catches some of his best smallmouths in the mid-pool area.

If the stream bottom in the middle of the pool has sections of cobblestones you can expect to find many madtoms here. These minnows rank high on the list of favorite foods for big smallmouths. Chub minnows are found in the middle of those pools that have a strong current. I use the Murray's Madtom to match the natural madtoms and Shenk's White Streamer and the Murray's Chub to match the chubs.

The across-stream streamer technique is productive to use in the mid-pool area unless the current is exceptionally fast. In fast currents I use a technique I call "sweeping a streamer" to help me run my flies deeper. That is, I cast up and across stream at a forty-five-degree angle and after the streamer sinks deeply I sweep it slowly along the bottom of the pool.

Gravel Bars

The shallow gravel bars along the river banks and islands are the natural habitat of many schools of shiner minnows. The bass often prowl along the edges of these areas in water three or more feet deep and quickly grab any minnows that leave the safety of the shallows.

Gravel bars hold many shiner minnows and the bass feed around them during the day and over them at dusk and dawn.

I've had great success with students in my fly-fishing schools by having them fish these areas with streamers such as the Silver Outcast and Murray's Shiner. During very low light levels the bass move out onto the gravel bars and chase the minnows, affording very exciting target-shooting-type fishing as you attempt to accurately cast your fly out in front of the cruising bass.

Undercut Banks

Some of the most consistent fishing in many smallmouth rivers can be found along the banks. The shade from large trees or undercut banks found here apparently give the bass a feeling of security and they are willing to feed all day. Any landborne food such as mice, frogs, grasshoppers and crickets that accidently tumble into the river are falling right onto the dinner tables of the bass.

Undercut banks can be both the feeding stations and homes for some of the largest bass.

When you find a shaded bank with water from hip to chest deep over a cobblestone stream bottom you can expect good fishing with surface bugs. If the water is deeper than this show them a streamer.

Downfalls

If there is one way to improve the fish-appeal, and thus the fishing, along the banks we've just discussed it would be to topple a downfall into the river right beside the bank. The overhead protection and shade the downfall provides pulls the bass like a magnet.

The author shows the ideal across-and-downstream angle to fish a downfall with a surface bug in order to have control of the bug's drift.

I go out of my way to fish downfalls and devote extra time to them to be sure every bass there gets to see my fly—and they seldom let me down. Often I'll cover the whole area thoroughly with a surface bug then repeat the pass with a nymph or streamer just to play it safe. Tip: be sure to get your flies well back under the downfall because some large bass don't like to pull out very far to take their food.

Bank grassbeds

Many minnows and nymphs live in aquatic grassbeds and the bass can often be found feeding along the edges of bank grassbeds.

Grassbeds along the banks are easy to fish and can usually be depended upon to yield several good smallmouths.

An ideal way to fish them is to wade downstream parallel to the grassbed and cast across and slightly downstream so your bug or fly falls about a foot from the grass. Often the strike comes right away so be ready to set the hook instantly. If you don't get a strike, *slowly* swim your fly out expecting the strike at any moment. Bring it out about ten feet then pick it up and cast it about five feet further down the grassbed.

Ledge Grassbeds

Ledge grassbeds are a reservoir of food for the bass while the deep water close by gives the bass great protection. The bass can cruise along the edges of the grass and up into the open pockets and easily pick off a meal in a hurry.

An effective way to fish ledge grassbeds is with a surface bug and thoroughly search out all of the grass-river interfaces where the water is over two feet deep.

Lefty Kreh is a master at fishing ledge grassbeds and catches many large smallmouths from these areas each year.

These ledges often run across the rivers giving us many options as to how to approach and fish them. However, my favorite method is to approach them from straight up the river and cast down to them or to come in below them and cast straight upstream to the grassbeds. Whichever route you choose try to thoroughly fish all of the edges of the grassbed.

Submerged Grassbeds

Late in the summer submerged grassbeds hold some of the largest smallmouths. They contain a great amount of food and the bass apparently like the overhead cover and shade they provide.

I've had many days when the bass in the open water were so wary it was difficult to get within casting distance of them. Then I'd move into the submerged grassbeds and get outstanding fishing.

One effective technique is to fish surface bugs in the open bays within the grassbeds and along the edges where the grass meets the open water along the sides. I've had great success with this technique for the students in my schools.

A slightly different tactic is extremely effective if, for some reason, the bass are preferring to feed underwater. We sometimes find this if the water is four to six feet deep along the edges of the grassbeds. When I find this I like to wade upstream as close to these deep areas as the stream depth permits. I cast a weighted fly such as an Olive Strymph upstream and after giving it time to sink deeply I strip it very slowly back downstream along the stream bottom. I've had great success with this tactic late in fall when the cool water prompts bass to hold deeply.

Gentle Tails of the Pools

You can often find many feeding bass in the gentle pool tails during low light levels, such as dusk and dawn, and on heavily overcast days. There are great populations of minnows around the cobblestones here and fishing a Shenk's White Streamer or a Murray's Madtom across this area can give you some fast action. I fish often in the evenings after I close my fly shop and frequently I'll stop wherever I'm fishing and head to the tails of the pools to fish the last half hour of daylight.

Jeff Murray catches some of his largest bass from submerged grassbeds.

The concentration of food in the tails of many pools attract the bass to feed there.

The fishing is often so good that each evening the anticipation of what I'll find is tremendous.

I usually start about two hundred feet above the tail of the pool and slowly and methodically fish my way down to the very end of the pool. If the current is moderately fast I'll stay with the streamers mentioned above. If the specific pool tail is fairly slow and not over three feet deep I'll often fish surface bugs with great success. The surface game is often very fast and very exciting.

Ledge Tails of the Pools

In order to understand how the bass feed in front of these ledges, and how you can effectively fish these areas, look at these ledges as being dams which momentarily slow the currents. This buffer zone gives bass an ideal feeding station on which they can hold with very little effort. If the upstream face of this ledge is vertical, or even better slightly undercut, the largest bass in the area will frequently feed here.

Large bass often hold immediately in front of the ledges that form the tails of some pools where they feed on the minnows and nymphs the stream delivers to them.

I like to wade in below these ledges and cast upstream or slightly up and across stream with a weighted nymph or streamer. After allowing it to sink deeply, I strip it back downstream along the stream bottom. The strike usually comes when the fly approaches the ledge. It is important to keep a tight line on the fly as it drifts back downstream so you can feel the strike.

Chapter 5

Minnow-Matching Tactics

Smallmouth bass feed heavily upon minnows, small fish, crawfish and leeches simply because there are so many of them in our streams.

The most prevalent minnows that are available to the bass are shiners, chubs, sculpins and madtoms. There is some overlap in the natural habitats of these minnows, but basically they live in different parts of the rivers, they act differently and look different. These different characteristics are what we need to take advantage of with our tactics and fly patterns in order to be consistently successful in catching smallmouths.

As a youngster growing up on the North Fork of the Shenandoah River I used to seine these minnows to use as bait in my own fishing and to sell to the adult fishermen in my area. I knew exactly where I could find the different minnows and how they acted. Later when I started fly-fishing for smallmouths this basic knowledge was invaluable. Even today, it guides me in the selection of the specific flies to use in different parts of the river and the best tactics to use.

Shiner minnows are so well liked by smallmouth bass they often go out of their way to feed on them. Photo by Rob Simpson.

In order for you to take advantage of this "minnow matching" approach, let's break these minnows down into three groups, depending on the depth of the water in which we normally find them. We'll look at those living in the shallows first, then the ones that live in the deeper water, and finally the minnows that live on the stream bottom.

Shiner Minnows

The shiner minnow is a schooling minnow that lives over the shallow gravel bars in water from six inches to two feet deep throughout much of the season. Once the aquatic grassbeds form in the summer many shiners can be found throughout the grassbeds.

Shiners on the Gravel Bars

Some of the largest smallmouth bass the students in my schools catch come from the simple method of fishing a shiner imitation, such as a Silver Outcast, along the drop-offs where the shallow gravel bars along the sides of the river taper off into the three- to four-foot-deep water in the main parts of the river. This is easy to achieve if you stay thirty to forty feet back from the edge of the drop-off so as not to scare the bass.

I like to wade slowly down the river and cast a Silver Outcast across and slightly downstream so it falls about ten feet out beyond the drop-off then strip it slowly across this interface. Large bass often cruise these areas on the look out for any shiners that stray out from the shallows and they will grab our flies as soon as they see them. By slowly wading down the whole gravel bar and making each successive cast about five feet further downstream you can usually take several nice bass along the edge of each gravel bar.

These bass holding in close to the edges of the gravel bars are often very wary so you should resist the urge to wade all the way out to the river edges of these gravel bars to fish the rest of the river further out. Once these bass are spooked it may be a half hour or more until they move back in. I've adopted a standard method with which I fish all the way down the gravel bar, staying well back from the drop-off. If I want to fish the main part of the river further out I get out of the river and walk back upstream then go out into the river and fish the depths with possibly a deeper-running shiner pattern like a Clouser's Shiner or a Murray's Shiner.

Shiners in the Grassbeds

As the aquatic grassbeds form throughout the rivers during summer, many shiner minnows move into them, apparently attracted by the security they provide. Smallmouths are quite aware of the minnows here and feed heavily on them in and around the grassbeds.

Many large bass cruise the deep water along the edges of grassbeds where they pick off any shiner minnows that stray too far from home.

I get very excited when I find aquatic grassbeds that look like the ones pictured above. This enthusiasm comes from a lifetime of getting great fishing in these areas and I fully expect to find cooperative fish as I approach them. Simply stated, these grassbeds seldom let me down.

Due to the abundance of shiners in these grassbeds I consider them to be prime feeding areas for large bass. But then when I see the four- to five-foot-deep cuts close by I realize these can easily be the homes for many large bass. Consequently we have a choice location where the bass can find great quantities of food within a few feet of home.

My goal is to cast my fly about every two feet all around these grassbeds!

An effective technique is to wade upstream and cast upstream so the streamer drops about a foot from the grass. Strip it out very slowly about ten feet then pick it up and cast it to a new spot several feet further along the grassbed. If the water is less than three feet deep I prefer the Silver Outcast. If the water is over three feet deep, I use the Murray's Shiner or Clouser Silver Shiner because these two streamers are weighted, making it easy to fish them deeply.

In order to fish the upstream side of these grassbeds I wade around the ends of them until I'm slightly above them which gives me a good angle to fish across stream and swim my streamer parallel to the grassbeds. If, however, the river is low and I suspect the bass are wary I wade about fifty feet above them and cast down and across to them at about a twenty-degree angle and slowly strip my fly out. Regardless of the angle I choose to fish the upstream side of these grassbeds, my goal is always the same—use a very cautious approach and cast my streamer in as tight to the grass as I can get it.

Aquatic grassbeds that grow along the banks of the rivers often extend out into the stream twenty to thirty feet and may reach several hundred feet downstream. These also hold great populations of shiner minnows, and they are actually the easiest to fish effectively of all the grassbeds.

A very effective way to fish the bank grassbeds is to wade downstream parallel to them about forty feet out in the river and cast a Silver Outcast streamer right against the grass. Get tight to the fly as soon as it touches the water because the strike often comes within the first several seconds—these bass are here to feed. If you don't get the strike right away, slowly strip it out about ten feet then pick it up and cast it several feet further down the grassbed. By wading slowly down the river and systematically fishing the grassbeds in this way you can easily take many nice bass from each grassbed.

Chub Minnows

Chub minnows are the most broadly distributed minnows in many smallmouth rivers. They are not schooling minnows, but where you find one you usually find many more and the bass seem to be constantly on the lookout for them and will take a well-fished chub imitation in many locations.

Most chubs are robust silver minnows that look amazingly like tiny tarpon. They are strong swimmers which helps them adapt well to many locations throughout the rivers. You will find them below riffles, in heavy runs, and in the cuts between ledges.

My favorite chub minnow imitations are Shenk's White Streamer, White Zonker and Murray's Chub all in sizes 4, 6, and 8.

Some of the easiest bass to catch are those that feed on chubs below the riffles.

A trick I learned from Charley Waterman for fishing the water below riffles for trout on large western rivers has been a great help to me in my smallmouth fishing. Many large bass feed on chubs in the very upper corners of the pools close to the bank right where the riffles empty into pools. In low light levels, the bass might feed here for much of the day, but since the water is only several feet deep they are very wary, requiring that we use a cautious approach.

For example, I like to stay about ten feet back on the bank and make my first cast only about twenty feet across the riffle and let the current sweep my streamer into this corner where I impart a very slow line hand stripping action. My second cast is about ten feet further out and I fish this back slowly. This technique has

Chub minnows are present in many areas in most smallmouth rivers and the bass feed heavily upon them. Photo by Rob Simpson.

given me many large bass that I would have scared if I would have waded into the river before starting to fish.

After covering the corner thoroughly I'll wade into the edge of the pool and fish the main part of the river where the riffle enters the main part of the pool. The largest bass here will seek out boulders or crevasses in the bottom of the river to find protection from the force of the current. With this in mind I always try to spot these feeding stations before moving very far out into the river to make my presentation. I use polarized glasses and a hat with a dark underneath side of the brim and try to see these areas. The boulders appear as a different color from the stream bottom around them and the crevasses are a dark shade.

Once I've spotted these feeding stations I wade into a casting position which places them down and across stream from me at a forty-five-degree angle about forty feet away. I cast my streamer about ten feet upstream and ten feet beyond it. I feel this angle of presentation is very important because it gives the streamer time to sink deeply as it approaches the feeding station and it gives me time to get in complete control of the drift. Now I can slowly strip the fly across in front of the bass holding in these areas, and I can instantly feel the strike and set the hook.

It is imperative here, and with any technique when fishing an underwater fly across and downstream, to keep the rod tip pointed *where the fly line comes out of the water*. This simple step enables you to feel the strike the instant the bass takes your fly and it gives you the full sweep of the fly rod which helps in setting the hook quickly before the bass detects it as a phony and ejects it—you have only about a second to a second and a half. This basic rod-handling technique has often helped the students in my schools to double the number of fish they catch when fishing streamers.

Another simple manipulation often helps improve our results when fishing streamers. I like to try to have my streamer come across the stream broadside to the current as much as possible. Realizing that the bass face directly into the current as they hold on a feeding station, this enables me to swim my fly broadside in front of them showing them a big mouthful which they may not be able to resist.

Unfortunately the currents that the fly line is riding upon are often considerably faster or slower than those in which the fly is drifting. This means we must reposition the fly line in order for the fly to act the way we want it. We may need to "mend" the fly line either upstream or downstream in order to achieve the fly action we desire. However, try to never move the fly as you mend the line or you will pull it up off the stream bottom and possibly away from the waiting bass. And always pick up the slack with your line hand which you mended into the cast so you can *feel* the strike. Think of "mending" a cast as "correcting" the drift in order to make the fly behave the way you want it to. Only mend the line when the fly is not acting the way you prefer.

Fishing the upper reaches of the pools with a chub imitation will enable you to catch many large bass, as the author shows.

Wading slowly down the river and fishing a chub streamer in this way is one of the most dependable tactics you can use. Just be alert to locate the protected feeding stations around the boulders, ledges and crevasses.

Bottom-Hugging Minnows

Sculpins and madtoms, both of which live under stones ranging from softball to basketball size on the bottom of the rivers, are important foods for smallmouths. The sculpins prefer well-aerated water which means we often find the largest numbers in the riffles. Madtoms prefer slightly slower currents and thus find suitable homes in many parts of the river.

As youngsters seining sculpins to use for bait, we'd always go to the riffles. We'd plant the seine and while one person held it in place the other fellow would stir the rocks upstream with an old broom handle. Lifting the seine would usually reveal enough sculpins to fish with all day. To catch madtoms we'd go out at night and with one person on each side of the seine we'd wade slowly upstream over the heads, sides and tails of the pools over cobblestone bottoms. Although I did not realize it at the time, this basic understanding of these two minnows has helped me greatly in my smallmouth fly-fishing. It taught me where the minnows were located, how they acted in the river and thus how to design effective matching streamers and how to fish them.

When the wildflowers bloom along the rivers many large bass feed heavily on minnows and we can catch them with streamers.

In order to get good fishing on your smallmouth rivers let's look at the different areas where these minnows are found and the tactics that are effective in each area.

Sculpins

In most smallmouth rivers there are more sculpin minnows in the riffles and immediately below them than in all of the rest of the pool combined. In low light levels, such as at dusk and dawn and on heavily overcast days, many large bass will move up into the two- to three-foot-deep parts of the riffles to feed. And there are always some smaller bass feeding here.

For this reason I always start fishing sculpin streamers well up in riffles that have large cobblestones on the stream bottom. An effective technique is to wade

Sculpin minnows are a great food source for smallmouth. Fish your streamers slowly along the stream bottom below the riffles.

into the river right where the riffle empties into the main part of the pool, make the first cast about thirty feet long and after giving the streamer time to sink, strip it back slowly—about six inches every ten seconds. The bass are feeding on natural sculpins on the stream bottom here and a slow retrieve helps keep the streamer close to the stream bottom.

From this same casting position I'll make several more casts, each successive cast about five feet longer than the previous one until I've covered all of the water I can control from this spot. This is a very effective method because as the current swings the streamer down and across stream its cutting a larger arc thus giving every bass out there a chance to see it.

At this point I have two options as to how to proceed. If the river is shallow enough I'll often wade all the way across the river fishing my way as I go. If, on the other hand, the water is too deep to wade across the river, I'll wade down the side of the pool several feet at a time and continue this same overlapping streamer casting tactic. This method and the sculpin streamers are usually effective for the first one hundred feet below the riffles. At this point we're approaching the part of the river that has more madtoms than sculpins, so I'll continue the same streamer-fishing tactics, but I switch to a madtom streamer.

My favorite sculpin streamers are Clouser's Sculpin, Shenk's Sculpin and Whitlock's Sculpin all in sizes 4, 6, and 8.

Madtoms

Madtoms are true minnows although they look like baby catfish. This was the favorite bait used by the serious bait-fishermen on the Shenandoah River when I was growing up in the fifties. Each year the largest six or eight smallmouths in the local "big fish contest" were always caught on madtoms.

My two favorite madtom streamers are Murray's Madtom and Whitlock's Hare Water Pup both in sizes 4 and 6.

Let's look at the three areas where you can expect to find bass feeding on natural madtoms, and the tactics that are productive:

About a hundred feet below the riffles which enter the heads of many pools there are good populations of madtoms if there are cobblestones on the stream bottom. The same across-stream tactics for fishing sculpins are effective here except we switch to madtom streamers.

The deep mid-pool areas often hold many madtoms if the stream bottom has some scattered cobblestones. I fish these areas with two different tactics I select based on the speed of the current and the depth of the pool.

If the mid-pool area is less than five feet deep and there is a slow to moderate current rate I use the same across-stream tactic we've just been discussing except that I allow longer for the madtom streamer to sink deeply before retrieving it slowly across the stream bottom.

If the pool is more than five feet deep I switch to a moderately fast sink-tip fly line. I get my best results with those in which the first ten to fifteen feet sink at a rate of 2.5 inches per second to 4.25 inches per second. A nice thing about a sink-tip fly line is that the casting, fishing and strike detection is much the same as with a floating line.

However, since the flies are now running much deeper than with a floating line I do make a few changes.

I always use a five-foot leader in order to take full advantage of the sink-tip of the line. Remember, the way a sink-tip line gets the fly deeper is that first the line tip sinks which pulls the leader down then the leader pulls the fly down. So you can see if you would use a nine-foot leader like you use on a floating line you would nullify the advantage of the sink-tip line.

If you are a fly fisherman who would really like to catch some large bass on a fly, choose streamers that match these madtoms.

The slower and deeper you fish a madtom streamer the more large bass you'll catch. Natural madtoms are bottom-hugging minnows so this is where the bass are accustomed to feeding on them.

I also use special care when I'm using a sink-tip line to be sure I keep the rod tip pointed at the spot where the fly line leaves the water when I strip the streamers across the stream. This helps me feel the bass's strike which may seem softer with all of the extra line under water.

When I feel the bass take my fly I set the hook more vigorously with a sink-tip line than I do with a floating line. I strike firmly with a strong uplifting motion with my rod arm while simultaneously imparting a sharp jerk with my line hand. This extra effort helps assure that my strike is telegraphed all the way through the sunken fly line, so the bass is securely hooked.

I'll often devote an extra half hour to fishing a large deep mid-pool area with the across-stream slow stripping tactic with a Murray's Madtom on a sink-tip fly line because I know I'm showing my streamer to every bass on the bottom.

Several years ago two youngsters opened my eyes to a great potential for fishing my madtom streamers which I had previously not taken advantage of. These kids were using coffee cans with both ends removed to capture live madtoms in the tail of a pool on the North Fork of the Shenandoah River right behind my fly shop at Edinburg. They would roll over a softball-size rock in water a foot deep and instantly slam the open end of the coffee can down on the stream bottom where the rock had been. Their speed and the discolored water must have been the key to their ploy because they sure caught a lot of madtoms.

Since that day I've cashed in on some great madtom fishing in these areas. In order for you to take advantage of this great fishing in your streams let's look at how to identify these areas and the tactics that are productive.

The most productive pool tails I've found to fish with madtoms are those ranging from four feet deep in the middle of the river to two feet deep close to the bank. Those with basketball-size rocks out in the middle with gradually smaller size rocks down to softball size as they taper up to the banks have very large madtom populations. The last one hundred feet of the pool tails usually produce the most large bass, however, they will frequently be found all the way out to the sides of the pools here in the tails.

These areas definitely fish best early in the mornings, and late in the evenings, or when the water is slightly discolored or on very heavily overcast days.

I like to approach these pool tails from below. If the river is one hundred and fifty feet wide or less I start in the middle of the river. If the river is wider than this I start about one hundred feet off the bank which has the stone bottom composition discussed above.

The best tactic I've found is to wade up through the riffle where it leaves the pool until I can cover all of the lower portion of the pool tail—frequently I'll actually be standing in the upper part of the riffle to fish the pool above.

I make my first cast straight upstream about thirty feet and strip my madtom back along the stream bottom so it's moving just slightly faster than the current. This simplifies strike detection because with this tight line I can instantly feel the strike and set the hook. Successive casts are a little longer and fanned out to the right and left at about a forty-five-degree angle until I've comfortably covered all of the water I can reach from that casting position. Next I wade about ten feet over toward the side of the river I plan to fish and a few steps further up into the pool.

By selecting fly patterns, such as a Murray's Madtom, that look like real madtoms, and using tactics that make these flies act like real madtoms, one can catch many of the largest smallmouths.

Carefully fishing the tails of the pools with an upstream approach to swim a madtom streamer along the stream bottom will give you great action.

Here I repeat the up and up-and-across stream casting pattern in order to cover all of the water within reach.

I eventually fish my way over toward the side of the river until I can drift my flies right along the bank. If the water along the bank is over knee deep and there is a cobblestone bottom you can expect to get fast action so cover this thoroughly, while wading carefully so you don't scare the bass. In some pool tails this good fishing may continue for a hundred and fifty feet up along the banks.

These areas are so productive that I'll often devote over an hour to fishing each one.

Sunfish Streamers

The bait-fishermen on the Shenandoah River fifty years ago knew that smallmouth bass fed heavily on small sunfish. I found this out as a youngster by accident when one of the local old-timers I was fishing with on the river ran out of bait. He gave me his minnow bucket and key to go back to town to his locked minnow box in his spring and get him some more madtoms out of the left side of the minnow box. By mistake I opened the right side of his minnow box and to my surprise it contained several dozen two- to three-inch-long sunfish. I promptly locked it back and got the madtoms out of the other side of the box and took about a dozen to the river for the gentleman. When I told him I had accidently opened the wrong side of the minnow box and saw all of those sunfish he was furious even though I apologized for my mistake. I don't think he was mad because I saw he was using a bait that was illegal, but because I had discovered his "secret bait" that enabled him to catch more large bass than most of the other fishermen on the Shenandoah River.

My favorite two sunfish streamers are the Murray's Sunfish and the James Wood Bucktail.

A very productive area to fish these sunfish streamers is the shallows along the banks. Many sunfish fry hold in this water from one to two feet deep over stream bottoms composed of pea-size gravel and the bass often roam these areas to feed on them. I wade down the rivers about forty feet out from these areas and cast my fly tight in against the bank and strip it out about ten feet then pick it up and cast it several feet further downstream. By wading slowly down the river and placing each successive cast further downstream along the bank I usually get great fishing.

A second section of the river that is exceptionally productive with sunfish streamers is the downstream end of an island. These areas provide ideal spawning

The Murray's Sunfish Streamer is a very productive fly to fish along the banks in the shallows where young sunfish are found.

Many smallmouth bass feed heavily on young sunfish throughout the rivers simply because there are such large populations of these fry available to them.

areas for sunfish and the babes hold here throughout most of the summer because the islands block the force of the river from their fragile bodies. This is an appealing feeding area for the bass because they can cruise the nearby deep water and pick off any young sunfish that stray far from home. My favorite way to fish the lower ends of these islands is to wade into the river to a spot off the lower end of the islands and cast upstream and up-and-across stream and cover the whole area with a slow stripping action.

Crawfish

In many smallmouth rivers, crawfish represent an important part of the diets of many bass. Crawfish are bottom-hugging creatures, making their homes in tiny tunnels they form under stream bottom rocks that range from softball up to basketball sizes.

My favorite crawfish patterns are those designed by Dave Whitlock, Bob Clouser and Barney Singer. These are all very productive when fished over the rocky stream bottoms with a slow darting action that mimics the action of a real crawfish dashing from the security of one boulder to the next.

This tactic is effective throughout the day, but I'd like to share with you something that happened to me one evening recently that has greatly improved my crawfish fishing.

My son Jeff and I were float-fishing the river in our Watermaster Kick Boats and I came to the take-out point at dusk about fifteen minutes before Jeff did.

Sitting there in my kick boat as I waited for him I noticed several crawfish scurrying around the stream bottom practically under my feet. Sitting quietly, I studied the stream bottom very carefully and was amazed to see the number of crawfish crawling around the rocks, apparently looking for something to eat. The darker it got, the more crawfish came out. This is something we can definitely take advantage of in our fishing.

Prompted by my experience that late evening on the river, I decided to experiment with my angling with crawfish patterns under various stream conditions at different times of the day.

Heavily overcast days will definitely give you better action with crawfish patterns than bright sunny days.

Slightly discolored water in the middle of the day is preferable to crystal-clear water at that time. A standard which I use in determining if the water is too discolored for good fishing is to look down at my feet when I'm standing in knee-deep water. If I can see my feet, I usually get good fishing. If I cannot see my feet the water is too discolored for good fishing.

Crawfish are a very rich food source for smallmouths and they seldom pass up any they can find.

If you definitely want to improve your fishing with crawfish patterns consider fishing from the last half hour of daylight on into the dark. The crawfish are out looking for their own food and many large bass feed heavily at dusk and in the dark.

Fly-fishing at night is not as difficult as one might assume. Here are some basic guidelines that I've found very helpful:

Fish a section of the river you already know so you have room for your back cast. Carefully plan where you will wade into the river and especially the exact

Jeff Murray gets great fishing with crawfish patterns in low-light levels when the natural crawfish are active.

spot you plan to get out of the river. I once had to climb up a steep, slippery, muddy bank laced with an old barbed wire fence in the dark because of poor planning—not only is this foolish, it's dangerous. Carry a small flashlight with which you can easily change flies and rework a leader if needed. A second larger flashlight for navigating the stream bank and hiking back to your car is a good investment. Apply a generous coating of insect repellent before you leave the car.

The tactics for fishing crawfish patterns at night are much the same as fishing them during the day, except that now you can expect to catch some large bass in shallower water than you would during the day. A method I've found very productive is to locate a cobblestone stream bottom in water from two to three feet deep along the banks and wade downstream about forty feet out to fish this across and slightly downstream. This angle lets me feel the strike instantly as I crawl my crawfish across the stream bottom.

Another good area to fish crawfish patterns at night is the heavy runs several hundred feet below riffles where the water is from four to five feet deep over a bottom having many basketball size rocks. The same across and downstream tactic used along the banks is good here. However, it often is necessary to use a moderately fast sink-tip fly line here.

Leeches

Leeches are found in the slow sections of many rivers, often in great numbers around aquatic grassbeds. Like crawfish they are most active in low light level, such as at dawn, dusk, on heavily overcast days, and in slightly discolored water.

Leeches swim with a very pronounced undulating action that I feel is important to imitate. Leeches vary greatly in color, but the most prominent colors are dark olive, dark brown and grayish-black. Flies tied in these colors with soft materials that can be brought to life easily as we fish them slowly are best. The Fur Leech, Bunny Leech and Marabou Leech are all excellent in sizes 4, 6, and 8. Dave Whitlock even told me that he thought the Murray's Hellgrammite is one of the best leech imitations we have.

If I find myself on a stretch of river at dusk that has thick patches of aquatic grass I often use leech-fishing tactics. That is, I wade upstream around the outside edges of the grassbeds and cast upstream so my fly falls within a foot or two of the grass. After it sinks deeply I use a bouncing retrieve to mimic the undulating swimming action of a real leech by lifting and dropping the rod tip as I retrieve the fly back downstream.

On very heavily overcast days natural leeches become very active, and I've had the fishing change from slow to outstanding in just a matter of minutes as a dense cloud cover moves in. Usually it will remain good as long as the overcast conditions last, so try to cash in on this.

Chapter 6

Fishing Nymphs For Smallmouths

Many anglers make impressive catches with Damselfly nymphs around aquatic grassbeds from June through September—a slow spurting action is very effective.

Fishing nymphs for smallmouth bass is very much like fishing large nymphs for trout in large western rivers. In fact, most of the refinements I use in my smallmouth nymph fishing I learned from the late Charlie Brooks of West Yellowstone, Montana when he kindly took me under his wing to fish the large trout rivers in the Rockies. Even the Murray's Hellgrammite, which is my most productive smallmouth nymph, is based on a design concept that Brooks showed me.

An extremely important approach in smallmouth nymphing is that one select or tie nymphs that can be made to "act like" the real nymphs in the stream because this action is what triggers a strike by the wise old bass. This holds true whether we're trying to mimic the undulating swimming action of the real hellgrammite or the spurting movements of a natural damselfly nymph.

Since many anglers are quite familiar with basic streamer-fishing methods let's first investigate the smallmouth nymph-fishing techniques that utilize a similar method.

Swimming Nymphs

Dragonfly Nymphs

Some low-gradient smallmouth rivers contain many large pools with stream bottoms composed of a mixture of sand, gravel and silt with a lacing of limestone ledges. If the water is over four feet deep in these pools, one can expect to find the bass feeding on the natural dragonfly nymphs that make their homes here.

A very effective tactic is to wade into the side of the river at the upstream end of this pool and cast a Dragonfly Nymph or a Casual Dress Nymph across stream, give it time to sink deeply then retrieve it slowly across the stream bottom with a four-inch darting action.

My first cast is about thirty feet out into the pool and I fish this back about ten feet. Each successive cast is about five feet longer until I'm reaching out about sixty feet. The stream current causes the nymph to swing downstream even as I strip it back slowly, so each cast drifts my nymph through a different part of the stream. After I complete this series of overlapping casts I wade downstream and repeat this tactic about every ten feet until I cover the whole pool.

Damselfly Nymphs

There are very large populations of damselfly nymphs in the grassbeds and brush piles in most smallmouth rivers and one can often find the bass feeding on these nymphs. These insects use the grass and bush beneath the water much like a ladder in order to climb to the surface of the stream where they pop their wings and fly away as adult insects. This activity, and especially the free-swimming nature of these nymphs, make them vulnerable to the bass. This swimming is in short one- to two-inch spurts, and this is the action I try to imitate with my artificial damselfly nymphs.

I use several different tactics to fish my Damselfly Nymphs depending upon the stream level because this influences how wary the bass are and how I can best approach them.

For example, from the time the grassbeds form in June until early August the rivers normally carry a good water level and the bass may not be exceptionally wary. During this period I wade downstream parallel to the grassbeds along the banks and cast my Damselfly Nymph down and across stream at about a ten-degree angle so it falls within a foot of the grassbed. I get tight to the fly quickly because often the strike comes within the first several seconds. If I do not receive the strike right away I strip my nymph out in spurting actions that mimics the natural movements of the real damselfly nymphs—a two-inch strip about every five seconds is very effective. I fish this out about ten feet from the grass then pick it up and cast it two feet further down the grassbed and repeat the stripping action. I wade slowly down the river and place each successive cast two feet further downstream until I've covered the whole grassbed.

Aquatic grassbeds that encircle many of the limestone outcroppings in mid-river hold many damselfly nymphs. These can be fished effectively from upstream by casting down and across stream to them and by wading across the river either above or below them and fishing straight out ahead of you. However, my favorite way to fish these grassy ledges is to wade in about sixty feet below them and fish upstream to them. This is especially effective in low, clear water late in the summer because I feel I do not spook as many fish with this upstream approach as I do with other methods.

If you find a deep cut that has an old downfall beside an aquatic grassbed you can expect it to hold a very large bass. Such was the case with one of the students in my smallmouth school. He had the bass follow a streamer, but refuse it on the first day of the school. The second day of the school he told his wife he really wanted to catch that bass. He cautiously climbed a high bank that enabled him to study the area where he had seen the bass. Finally spotting the bass close to the downfall he went way upstream, crossed the river and came back to try the bass. On the first cast he caught him on a Damselfly Nymph—a fly that looked like one of the staple foods for that bass in that specific area. It pays to be patient.

Swing Nymphing

This method of fishing nymphs enables me to fish them deeper than any method I've found with a floating line. I use this in the deep pools below the riffles and the deep cuts between river-crossing ledges, or for that matter almost anywhere that's real deep.

Charlie Brooks, the late nymph fishing expert of West Yellowstone, Montana, taught me this technique for fishing nymphs for trout on the large rivers in the Rockies. After several different names had been used to identify this technique we finally came to refer to it as the "Brooks method". In order to master the powerful currents in the largest rivers, Brooks used a custom-built, very fast-sinking, thirty-foot head fly line. Since our smallmouth rivers are not as fast as Brooks' trout rivers I've found that a floating line does an excellent job for us. I've also made a few changes in Brooks original method in order to fine-tune this system to our smallmouths and thus use the term "swing nymphing" to prevent confusion. Here is how it works.

First I identify the deep portion of the river I suspect will hold the bass. This could be the upper reaches of a pool where the incoming riffle empties into the

Swing nymphing: 1) The cast is made up and across stream at a forty-five-degree angle and the nymph is allowed to sink. 2) The rod is held up and out over the stream at a forty-five-degree angle and the slack line is stripped in with the line hand. 3) Swing the rod downstream ahead of the nymph and when you feel the strike, set the hook firmly with the rod and the line hand.

pool. The water may range from four to six feet deep over a stream bottom covered with bushelbasket-sized boulders. The bass hold close to the stream bottom protected by these boulders and grab any food that drifts by—however, the big bass will seldom pull up far from the stream bottom to grab this food. This means we should strive to drift our nymphs right along the stream bottom.

In order to achieve this depth with my nymphs my next step is to position myself right beside the area I plan to fish. My first cast is made up and across stream at about a forty-five-degree angle with about a twenty-foot cast. The nymph is allowed to sink deeply on a slack line, do not mend the line or pick up any slack at this stage because this will rob you of the depth you need. After your nymph is close to the stream bottom and starting to drift downstream extend the fly rod up and out over the stream at a forty-five-degree angle while simultaneously stripping in the extra slack line with your line hand. At this point you should have a tight line from the line hand all the way down to the nymph, but use care not to pull it up far off the stream bottom.

As the current drifts the nymph along the stream bottom rotate your body slightly downstream and, with the rod pointed up and out over the river at a forty-five-degree angle, swing it downstream at the same speed as the nymph is drifting. You should now have a tight line on the nymph as it drifts by straight out from where you are standing and you can feel the strike the instant the bass takes your nymph.

Good patterns for swing nymphing should be constructed so they look alive when just drifting with the current. Good examples are the Strymph, Murray's Ghost Nymph and Murray's Road Kill Nymph.

Make a conscious effort to set the hook quickly and firmly when you feel a strike. Quickly because you have only a second to a second and a half before the bass detects the nymph as a phoney and ejects it. Because of the downstream curve in the belly of the line that occurs with this method, you need to be sure your strike is telegraphed all the way down to the bass with enough force to set the hook. (Using barbless hooks and sharpening them often is also a great help in setting the hook.)

My second cast is made up and across stream at the same angle as the first cast, but about five feet longer. This will allow the nymph to drift down through the pool a little further out than the first cast. Each successive cast is made about five feet longer than the previous cast until you are covering all of the water out in the pool to about forty feet from where you are standing. Trying to cover water further out in the pool with this method is usually not productive because the currents between you and your nymph pull on the line and leader and rob you of the depth you need.

After covering this part of the pool you can wade downstream and at about every ten feet stop and repeat this swing-nymphing technique. This method allows your nymph to drift downstream in an overlapping pattern that practically assures you that every bass in front of you will see it.

Upstream Dead-Drift Nymphing

Fishing nymphs with the dead-drifting technique is entirely different from the swing nymphing method just discussed because here you are wading upstream, casting upstream and you are detecting the bass's strikes by *seeing* them on your indicator system. The Murray's Bright Butt Leader, with two Scientific Anglers Indicators covered in Chapter 2, is a great help in detecting the strikes.

Upstream dead drift nymphing: 1)The cast is made upstream from twenty to thirty feet. 2) The slack line is stripped in with line hand at the same rate the nymph drifts downstream. 3) Set the hook firmly with both the rod and the line hand when the bass takes the nymph.

Reading the water in order to identify where the bass will be holding and feeding is very important in order to be successful when fishing nymphs upstream with the dead-drifting method. The bass often hold on the stream bottom in the depressions around bushelbasket-size boulders in water ranging from two to four feet deep. Here they face into the current and intercept any nymphs that drift by. This is very effective when fishing Hellgrammites below riffles. Using polarized sunglasses I carefully look for these areas as I wade upstream. From twenty to thirty feet below them I cast my nymph straight up or up and across stream at a narrow angle to a spot about five feet upstream of the suspected holding water.

If the river is shallow enough I may wade back and forth below the riffles to fish with this method. If it's too deep for this I simply fish up my side of the river carefully reading the water for productive looking areas as I go.

Some anglers are reluctant to try upstream dead-drift nymph fishing for bass because they feel the need to see the basses' strikes rather than feel them makes this method too difficult to learn. Realizing this, I have developed a simple six-step approach that will help you master this method.

Six Steps For Mastering Upstream Dead-Drift Nymphing

1. Keep the fly line in your line hand on the presentation cast.
2. Keep the line hand within six inches of the rod hand on the presentation cast.
3. As the forward cast begins, use your line hand to place the line over the first or second finger of your rod hand.
4. When the forward cast turns over and is five to ten feet over the water strip in all of the slack with your line hand. This assures that you will have a tight line from your line hand to the nymph as it begins drifting back downstream.
5. Facing upstream, with the rod held at a forty-five-degree angle over the water, strip the line in with the line hand at the same rate the nymph is drifting back downstream. Watch the indicators or the fluorescent butt of the leader closely, when it stops you know you have a strike.
6. Set the hook quickly by lifting the rod sharply while simultaneously jerking back quickly with the line hand.

Emerging Nymphs

One of the most exciting times to fish nymphs for smallmouth bass is when they are feeding on natural nymphs swimming up from the stream bottom to emerge into adult insects. This occurs with several different mayflies and caddisflies and I use the same tactics with all of these hatches.

One of the most popular hatches is the white Miller (white fly) mayfly hatch. This is the *Ephoron leukon* and they are exceptionally numerous on some rivers, so I'll use this specific hatch to look at the tactics that are effective.

Natural Hellgrammites are an important food source for smallmouth bass, and the Murray's Hellgrammite is an exceptionally productive fly.

One especially effective tactic was developed by Jim Leisenring long ago for trout. The Leisenring lift is equally productive today for smallmouth bass. The nymph is cast up or up and across stream and allowed to sink deeply—the Red Squirrel Nymph size 10 is excellent on the white fly hatch. As the nymph drifts into the bass's suspected holding position the fly rod is lifted up in order to cause the nymph to swim to the surface just like a real emerging nymph. In some cases the strike comes when the nymph starts its asscent. However, I've had some bass chase a nymph to the surface and take it with a very splashy strike just as it is ready to leave the water. This tactic is very useful from an hour before the peak of the hatch on through the hatch.

Once I start seeing bass splashing about the surface as they are feeding on the natural emerging insects just an inch or two below the surface, I catch many fish with the sweeping-nymph tactic. I cast across stream to the area I see splashes, or generally cover the water if I do not see fish-feeding activity. The line is kept tight on the nymph and as the current sweeps the nymph downstream the rod is slowly lifted up and down about six inches every five seconds. By using an unweighted nymph and no weight on the leader, this pulsing fly action makes the fly look like a real insect struggling to emerge from the stream.

Cool, rich feeder streams that enter smallmouth rivers increase insect populations greatly.

With both of these tactics the takes are detected by feeling them since the line is tight from the line hand down to the fly.

As the hatch reaches its peak many bass continue to feed heavily upon the emerging nymphs in preference to the adult dry flies. However, at these times they often want our emerger drifting naturally with the current with no action imparted to it. The natural emergers are now within an inch or two of the surface of the stream and when a bass takes one its rise form looks very much like it's feeding on the natural dry flies drifting on the surface.

My favorite tactic at these times is to fish a dropper nymph below a dry fly. For example, in the white fly hatch I'll tie a size 12 Light Humpy on a 9-foot 3X leader and attach 20 inches of 3X tippet material to the bend of the dry-fly hook with an improved clinch knot. I attach a Red Squirrel Nymph size 10 to the tip of this with an improved clinch knot.

When I'm wading I fish this up or up and across stream to the areas I see rising bass. As this two-fly rig drifts back to me I watch the dry fly carefully for any slight movement signaling that a bass has taken my nymph and then I set the hook quickly.

This is also an excellent ploy to use when floating a river. Some beginning anglers have trouble detecting the basses' strikes on nymphs fished as a single fly. When we show them how to rig this dry-fly-and-nymph-dropper system they catch many bass by drifting these along the banks.

Late in the evening many bass feed heavily upon emerging nymphs, thus providing some of the most exciting fishing of the day.

Chapter 7

Taking Smallmouth On The Surface

The more I fish for smallmouth bass in many waters under a variety of conditions the more I find myself fishing for them on the surface. I'm sure part of this fascination comes from the fact that I enjoy seeing the bass come up and take my hard bugs, deer-hair bugs and dry flies, but I honestly believe that I often take more bass on the surface than I do under water.

This was just one of the three big bass this student took on the surface in the author's school.

I suspect there are traits in the genes of this gentleman of the warm water that motivates him to feed on the surface...I believe he actually enjoys it. For example, how else can one explain all of those smallmouths rising all around our drift boat to sip in adult caddisflies from the surface one late May evening when the water all around these bass was loaded with chub minnows which they could easily feed on. Was there more food value in the caddisflies? Of course not. Were the caddisflies easier to capture? Not really. Did the caddisflies taste better? You try them and then tell me, but I doubt it. I really believe those bass *enjoyed* feeding on the surface.

Will a really large bass come to the top to take a surface bug that, even when we use our largest bugs, are almost always smaller than our underwater flies? I can tell you from personal experience that they will. I believe this can be partly explained by the fact that, depending on the action we impart to our bugs, we can make them appear to the bass as being much larger than they actually are...a big mouthful you might say.

Where to Fish Surface Bugs

Fishing the surface for smallmouths is different from fishing under water because in the majority of cases we are fishing to bass that are located in areas that will easily let them grab any food that drifts by on top of the river—these locations are called *feeding stations*. Admittedly there are some locations in which a smallmouth's home is also an excellent feeding station. These are what I call "primary feeding stations", and they usually attract the largest bass in that part of the river. A logjam in three to four feet of water along a shaded bank is an excellent example of a primary feeding station.

Here are some of the features that contribute to surface-feeding areas that attract smallmouths. They will not all be found in each spot, but the more that are present in one specific location the more likely it will hold large bass.

Components of Good Surface-Feeding Stations

1. A good flow of food in a closeby current.
2. Something to block the force of the current.
3. Shade.
4. Water three to four feet deep.
5. Stream bottom composed of cobblestones or crevices in ledges.
6. Some of the best are close to banks, islands, aquatic grassbeds, ledge outcroppings, and log jams.

A very exciting part of fishing for smallmouth bass on the surface is drawing from the experiences you have had in the past and using these to try to figure out where and on what the bass will be feeding around the next turn of the river. In that there is a great amount of repetition in the makeup of all rivers, from one mile to the next, and from one river to the next this is a very successful approach.

The three types of patterns we use on the surface for smallmouths are hard-head bugs, hair bugs and dry flies. Since the hard-head bugs are the most popular we'll look at these first and then the other two.

Hard-Head Surface Bugs

Hard-head bugs are constructed with cork, hard foam, balsa wood or other similar buoyant materials. Some anglers refer to all of these as poppers and the popping action is indeed one way we can fish these bugs. However, there are many other actions we can produce with hard-head bugs. These actions are governed by the various manipulations we can impart to the bugs in conjunction with the influences of the currents upon the bugs. The cut of its face and the shape of the bug's body are the two physical characteristics that influence this action.

In order to distinguish between the styles of the three basic hard-head bugs let's give them names that are indicative of their basic actions.

The Chuggar is a robust body, deeply-cut-faced bug with which we can impart a very loud action. The Slider is a pointed-nose bug that we can use to produce a gentle action. The Popper is a flat-faced bug that is capable of a broad assortment of actions.

Fishing the Chuggar

This is the bug I use when I feel it is necessary to create extra commotion on the surface to get the attention of the bass.

Shenandoah Chuggar. The deeply cut face of the Chuggar enables the smallmouth angler to produce a loud action on the surface that can attract bass in heavy water.

Jeff's Chartreuse Chuggar landed within a foot of the bank. One sharp pull with the line hand was all that was needed to bring up the big bass.

Many bass hold in the upper reaches of the pools in water from two to four feet deep immediately below where the riffles enter the pools. Here they can easily pick off any struggling minnows or other natural foods the riffles push down into the pools.

A very effective tactic in this area is to wade into the river right where the riffle enters the pool and after casting a Chuggar straight across stream, strip it back with a loud strip-pause-strip retrieve. I use my line hand to strip the Chuggar about three feet, then I pause about ten seconds to allow it to drift with the current, then I strip it again. This produces an action the bass might perceive as a dying minnow struggling along the surface. If the depth of the water and the speed of the current permit, I like to wade all the way across the river using this tactic with my Chuggar. I like to use the gray-scaled Chuggar in this area because it has the general coloration of many of the minnows.

Other areas in which the Chuggars are a good bug to use are along shaded banks where the water is about five feet deep. This is not what I would consider ideal water for fishing surface bugs, but sometimes the bass surprise us. For example, recently my son Jeff and I were floating a smallmouth river in his Hyde drift boat, it was his turn to fish and I was at the oars. Jeff had taken several nice bass on his Chuggar along a shaded bank where the water was three feet deep, but as we turned a fast corner of the river the water became very deep. I wasn't expecting much surface action here, but the western bank was lined with giant oak trees that provided dense shade as the sun set behind them and I couldn't resist. I pulled hard on the oars to get Jeff within casting distance of the bank. His big Chartreuse Chuggar landed within a foot of the bank and Jeff gave it a sharp pull with his line hand that caused the bug to gurgle along the surface. A second strip was not needed because one of his largest bass of the summer sucked in the Chuggar and made three powerful jumps right beside us.

Many knowledgeable anglers consider Chuggars to be the choice surface bugs to use as darkness approaches in the evening. This is logical because the noise that we can produce with a Chuggar can easily attract bass that otherwise may not even be aware there is anything around to eat. At this time of the day I often fish a Chuggar anyplace in the river that is less than four feet deep and I usually find that a loud action is the most productive.

Fishing The Sliders

When I conduct our smallmouth bass fly-fishing schools on the Shenandoah River I get most of the students into more good fish with the Sunfish Slider than with any other fly or bug. I believe this is because it has great fish appeal and the students can quickly learn the best tactics for fishing it.

Sliders are pointed-nose, hard-head surface bugs that we go to when we want to produce a subtle teasing action in those areas where the bass are accustomed to feeding on the surface.

Most smallmouth rivers have many miles of river banks that produce outstanding fishing with Sliders. In order to locate these areas you want to look for stretches where the trees along the bank shade the river. You also want water that is three

Shenandoah Slider. The sleek design of the Slider helps us fish it with a tantalizing action in the slow shallow areas back under tree limbs where the bass find this action appealing.

to four feet deep over a river bottom covered with cobblestones or crevices in ledges. These are prime feeding stations and bass lying here let very little natural food get away from them.

This is why we should strive to make our Slider *act* like some living creature that has just tumbled into the river. Imagine, if you will, how a big natural moth would act if it accidently fell into the river a foot off the bank. It would flutter in the surface film for a few seconds then drift along with the current, then flutter again, then drift along. As you can well imagine it will not drift very far before a bass grabs it.

This is exactly what we try to achieve with our Sliders. I tell my students that they should try to make the Slider act like something good to eat and make it easy for the bass to capture. When this is achieved it is as close to a "sure thing" for catching smallmouth bass as I know.

Here is a technique for fishing Sliders against the banks that is exceptionally productive and very easy to master. Set yourself up so you are wading downstream parallel to the bank about forty feet from it. Cast down and across stream at a twenty-degree angle so your Slider drops onto the stream about a foot from the bank. Instantly extend you fly rod up and out over the stream at a forty-five-degree angle as far as you can reach. Right away mend the line upstream with just enough force to move the Slider only an inch or two. This mend is very important for not only does it bring life to the Slider, but by flipping the belly of the fly line upstream it delays the dragging force of the current on the line that would otherwise pull the

The author's students find that by making the Slider act like something good to eat, but easy to capture, they can catch many large bass.

Slider away from the bank immediately. Let the Slider drift naturally with the current right along the bank about five feet then mend the belly upstream again just enough to make the bug move slightly. After three or four mends and drifts, wade downstream about ten feet and repeat the sequence.

There are several aspects of this technique I should alert you to: This method is so effective that often the bass's strike comes within the first several seconds so be ready to set the hook quickly. Also, experience has shown me that the largest bass often prefer the most gentle bug-action. For this reason, when I'm using this method I frequently remind myself that I do not want to impart much motion to the Slider, but rather let it drift naturally with the current and just sort of flutter as it drifts along.

This method of fishing a Slider gently along the banks is equally effective whether you are wading or floating the river.

I've experimented with many color Sliders and find the sunfish (yellow) color the best with chartreuse coming in second.

Fishing the Popper

The true popper is a flat-faced tapered bug that enables us to impart a variety of actions thus making it useful in many situations. Although not as loud as a Chuggar, nor as subtle as a Slider, I find myself using them often. I can't explain the reason, but the light blue color is much more productive than any other color, with the damsel (mottled dark gray) color coming in second. These colors are so dependable that I use them for over ninety percent of my popper fishing.

Logjams in water less than four feet deep are very productive areas to fish Poppers. Frequently a spring flood will undercut the roots of a standing large oak tree right beside the river causing it to fall into the river. The roots still tether it to the bank while the powerful current pivots the top portion of the tree downstream.

This now provides one of those prime feeding areas we discussed where the resting area and the feeding station are very close together—you might say the bedroom is right beside the dining room.

My favorite way to fish a logjam with a Popper is to wade downstream to within forty feet of the uppermost part of the log about forty-five degrees out from it. My first cast drops the Popper right where the roots meet the bank. I give it a gentle popping action without moving it far away from the log. I actually want the current to drift it along right in front of the log because many bass hold in the shade of these logs and grab anything that drifts by. After my popper has drifted several feet I give it two gentle pops. With a little practice you will be able to fish the entire

Shenandoah Popper. Poppers are versatile bugs that can be fished with different actions making them useful in many areas. The Blue Shenandoah Popper is the author's favorite.

upstream face of a logjam in this way by gradually wading downstream as you fish it. When you hook a bass under a logjam try to quickly fight it away from the jam and land it in the open water. This prevents it from scaring the other bass under the logjam. In this way you may be able to catch several nice bass from each area.

Aquatic grassbeds that extend above the surface of the river around ledge outcroppings and along the banks are important feeding areas for smallmouths. These areas rank close to the top as my favorite sections of the river to fish with poppers simply because they seldom let me down.

When I find grassbeds around ledge outcroppings in the middle of the river I like to approach them from downstream and cast my popper up tight against the grass. There are great numbers of natural damselflies around the grass so I usually use the Shenandoah Damsel Popper size 6. I stay about forty to fifty feet below the grass and gradually wade across the river casting my popper about every three feet along the grassbed. I get tight to the popper right away because often the strike comes within the first several seconds. I allow the popper to lie still for about five seconds then give it two slow pops with my line hand and allow it to rest again for five to ten seconds. I continue this pop-pause-pop sequence to fish the popper about ten feet from the grass, then I pick it up and cast it several feet further along the grass. I find that by devoting my time to fishing close to the grass I catch many more bass than I do by fishing the open water way out from the grassbeds.

Often, after covering the downstream side of a grassbed, I wade around it and fish the upstream side with this same tactic. However, on the upstream side the bass are looking at me so I make longer casts and I wade very cautiously as I move along.

Aquatic grassbeds are great areas to fish with poppers. The abundance of natural food here attracts the bass and they often take our bugs as soon as they land on the water.

The aquatic grassbeds along the river bank are also great places to fish with poppers. In fact, in the mornings and evenings when the trees along the banks shade these areas they are even better than the grassbeds in mid-river. I use the same pop-pause-pop tactic here that I use around grassbeds in the middle of the river.

Brush piles that floods wash into the rivers are gold mines for popper action if they are in water from three to five feet deep. These may range from card-table-size to automobile size. Shiner minnows and damselfly nymphs live around the

Brush piles are the natural habitat for many minnows and nymphs and you can often catch several good bass around each one.

underwater maze and adult damselflies emerge onto and rest on that portion above the water. I've had some great action by fishing my poppers all around these brush piles, it's not at all unusual to catch several large bass from each one.

Let me tell you about an entirely different area that I've had such great success with when using poppers. In fact, I'm constantly on the lookout for these when I'm on a new river and go out of my way to fish them thoroughly. I'm referring to the downstream protected sections of the river below peninsulas coming out from river banks and below islands.

I find the bank peninsulas the most productive, and I suspect this is due to the shade the trees on the bank provide to these areas.

Envision, if you will, a small spit of river bank extending twenty to thirty feet out into the river. Over the years the force of the current swinging from the outermost point of this dry land has cut back into the bank below it. There is now a good moderate current that pushes back toward the bank for about a hundred feet below the peninsula. The water is waist deep over a clean cobblestone bottom. Often the main current pushing down the middle of the river is extremely fast in these sections of the river and the bass move to these protected sides to feed.

These are such dependable hot spots that I like to fish my popper over practically every square foot of water here; I want to be sure that every big bass sees my bug.

In order to do this I wade into the river about a hundred and fifty feet below these peninsulas and get about thirty feet off the bank. From this position I can

Deer-hair bass bugs can be tied to imitate a variety of smallmouth foods and many experienced anglers carefully select the one that matches the natural food in the area they plan to fish.

cover all of the water from the bank out about sixty feet into the river as I wade and fish slowly upstream. It is not at all unusual to catch several large bass from each of these areas so as soon as I hook one I quickly work it down to me or out into the main part of the river so its fighting and jumping will not scare the other large bass behind the peninsula. Be sure to fish these areas all the way upstream to the main flow of the river because often some of the largest bass will be there. Once you learn to identify these feeding stations and get the great action they can give you, you'll never pass one up.

Deer-Hair Bass Bugs

The hollow nature of deer body hair enables us to tie a broad variety of surface bugs that are very effective for smallmouth bass. The standard hair bugs include such highly effective patterns as the Whitlock Bugs, Tapply Bugs and the Shenandoah Series. The Dahlberg Bugs have cleverly designed sculptured faces that enable us to impart a variety of different actions to them. Creative tyers can stack, pack and trim the deer-hair bug bodies to create very realistic mice, frogs and moths.

All of these bug styles are productive and since the bass often have an unexplained preference for one over the other I carry a variety at all times. My favorites tend to be those that have smooth streamlined designs with a minimum of appendages sticking out to the sides. This design is easy to cast and I've always felt I can cast this type of light deer-hair bug further than I can a hard-head bug of the same size.

As the rivers drop late in the summer and the water becomes very clear, the bass become exceptionally wary and punching out a little longer cast can make the difference between a so-so day and a memorable trip. One of the most dependable parts of the river I've found to fish deer-hair bugs in these low, clear streams are the long, flat pools with cuts in the stream bottom ledges from three to five feet deep. Many of these pools are over a hundred yards long and the surface may be as flat as a mirror. When you look at this type pool your first thought will probably be that there is no way you can wade to within casting distance of any worthwhile bass here without scaring it. Basically this is a correct assumption, but let me show you a way you might be able to tilt the odds in your favor.

I go to these pools the last hour of daylight and get in the river on the shaded western bank. I get about twenty feet off the bank and wade straight upstream. I punch out long casts concentrating on the water right along the bank. Many large bass hold around the tree roots, driftwood and undercut banks. The low light level in the evening and the natural overhead cover apparently make the bass feel more secure than they were just a few hours earlier because many of them take the bug before it has drifted a foot.

Fishing deer-hair bass bugs tight against the banks in the evening is a very effective tactic because many large bass feed heavily at this time.

An effective tactic to make the hair bugs look and act alive in this calm water is a pull-pause-pull action. With the rod tip pointed straight upstream at the bug, I use my line hand to pull the bug about a foot then pause about ten seconds and give it another pull. This repeated maneuver achieves two goals: it makes the bug act like a living creature and it maintains a tight line on it so you can easily set the hook when the bass takes the bug.

In addition to the water immediately beside the bank, I fan-cast out in front of me in an arc about twenty feet wide as I wade slowly upstream. If this water is waist to chest deep and there are crevices in a ledge bottom or bushelbasket-size rocks scattered along the stream bottom, the bass will often move here to feed at dusk.

The two points I constantly remind myself of when fishing this flat water is to wade very slowly upstream so I don't send out telltale waves ahead of me that would scare the bass and to make as long a cast as possible to reach beyond the area where I might scare the bass.

Some anglers believe they miss many of their strikes upstream on long casst because of the extra line on the stream. A technique I teach in my schools quickly enables even beginning anglers to master this problem. This involves setting the hook simultaneously with both the rod and the line hand as soon as the bass takes the bug. This helps you telegraph your strike quickly to the bass assuring a high percentage of hooked bass.

If the river levels are holding up well during the first several months of the season, the deer-hair mice, frogs and moths can be used to catch many bass along the river banks. Whether you are wading or floating the river, cast these bugs back tight against the banks where the bass are accustomed to seeing the naturals and you'll get great action.

Concentrate on those stretches where there are many tree limbs extending out over the river. Many creatures fall from the trees into the streams and the bass are accustomed to this and they will quickly grab a hair bug.

Real hot spots that can give you some easy bass are those twenty- to thirty-foot stretches where large tree limbs hang down to within less than a foot of the river. These shaded living-room-size bays back beneath the trees provide great feeding areas. On the first glance it appears that it would be impossible to get a hair bug back under these low-hanging limbs. However, not only can you achieve this, but you can catch many easy bass because they see very few flies or lures. A simple ploy is to cast your bug in tight against the bank in the closest opening in the limbs upstream of the congested area you want to fish. Do not retrieve your bug in the

Smallmouth bass will seldom pass up a natural wounded chub minnow struggling along the surface below old dams and you can expect to catch many of them there.

normal way, but, rather, allow the current to pull it back under the overhanging limbs, even feeding some slack line if needed. Once your bug is in the heavily shaded area impart a slow forward motion to it with your line hand to move it just several inches, then release the line and let the current pull it further downstream under the limbs. Quite probably you'll catch a bass before the bug drifts very far. Fight this bass out from under the limbs and after releasing it cast back up into the open area and let the current pull the bug even deeper under the limbs this time and repeat the bug action. It is not at all unusual to catch several good bass from each of these areas with this technique.

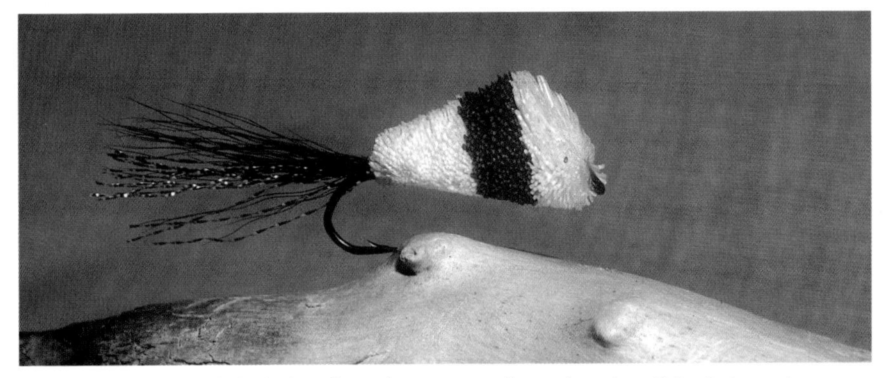

The Murray's Wounded Chub will catch many smallmouths when fished along the surface with an action that mimics a dying minnow.

Wounded Minnows

One of the easiest meals for a smallmouth to capture is a wounded or dying minnow struggling along the surface of the stream. These minnows drift helplessly along with the current, then with a spurt of energy they burst forward several inches in what is quite obviously a dying thrust. This short dash attracts the bass's attention and is our cue as to how we should fish our minnows to catch bass.

After a great amount of experimenting I found that a long, spun deer-hair streamer with an angled epoxy-coated concave face that looked generally like the prevalent minnows in each area did a good job for me. This series of Wounded Minnows has separate patterns to match shiners, chubs, sunfish and dace. The specific one I use depends on what I suspect the natural minnows will be in the part of the river I'm fishing.

For example, the Shiner Wounded Minnow is at its best around aquatic grass-beds and over the edges of gravel bars. The Chub Wounded Minnow is great below the riffles and in the tails of the pools. The Sunfish Wounded Minnows are very effective in the slow-water sections along the banks and especially in the back eddies. The Dace Wounded Minnows are at their best in the heavy runs.

The best action I've found to use with the wounded minnows is to give them two firm foot-long strips with the line hand. This causes them to dive beneath the surface and helps the epoxy face of the minnow create a sharp wobbling action. Pause from five to ten seconds to allow the minnow to bob back to the surface and drift with the current just like a real minnow would. Let it drift about ten seconds, then repeat the stripping and bobbing sequence.

This is a great tactic to use throughout the season in all normal water conditions. Even when the rivers are much more colored than normal I've taken some big bass with this method. I can only assume all of the racket I create on the surface quickly attracts their attention.

Dahlberg Hair Bugs

The Dahlberg Hair Bugs are a very cleaver design that can be fished with a great amount of diving and wiggling action due to their deeply sculptured faces. These are sometimes more effective than regular bugs when fished along the banks. Since it is impossible to determine when the bass will prefer this more active action I just experiment with them to see which works best on a given day in different stretches of the river.

The Dahlberg Diving Minnows are tied on heavier, longer hooks than the Dahlberg Bugs and can thus be used to mimic the actions of minnows.

The smallmouth bass that hold along the edges of grassbeds in water about three feet deep that is moving at a moderately fast pace are very susceptible to the Dahlberg Silver Diving Minnow. I get upstream of the edges of these grassbeds and cast downstream so the Diving Minnow falls about a foot from the edge of the grass. Using my line hand, I impart a very aggressive stripping action to the Diving Minnow that causes it to dive under the surface then I pause to allow it to come back to the surface. By continuing this diving and bobbing action all along the edge of these grassbeds you can take several nice fish from each grassbed.

The Dahlberg Diving Minnow is a very versatile fly that can give you good fishing in many areas. I enjoy experimenting with it using every action I can think of in many different parts of the river. I find the bobbing action mentioned earlier gives me many nice bass in the tails of the pools and below the riffles.

Deer-hair bugs, in general, are not designed to float as high on the stream surface film as hard-head bugs. In fact, I suspect this low-floating profile is the characteristic that often makes them so appealing to the bass, which explains why they out-produce the hard bugs on some days.

If you want to enhance the floating qualities of deer-hair bugs try massaging silicone cream into the hair portion of the bug's body when you start fishing. When the bug begins to get waterlogged as you use it and catch fish you can squeeze it out with your fingers and reapply more silicone cream.

In order to assure a high percentage of hooked fish on deer hair-bugs, whether you purchase them or tie your own, make sure there is adequate space between the point of the hook and the body of the bug. If there is not, you can easily trim the stomach of the bug with scissors or a single-edge razor blade, using care not to cut so deeply that you cut the tying thread.

Keep in mind that the more streamlined the deer-hair bug is, the smoother and easier it will cast. Appendages, such as legs and wings, that stick out very far at great angles to the bug's body can hamper smooth casting and may actually twist the leader tippet if they are not perfectly symmetrical. But since smallmouth bass tend to strike the head area of their prey you can have slim bugs with long streamlined tails that cast beautifully and catch bass like crazy.

Weed guards are fine on hair bug if there is a great amount of surface grass where you are fishing. However, I don't use bugs with weed guards unless I have to. A smallmouth angler I admired greatly always said, "weedless, fishless", implying that the weed guards may deflect some of the strikes and we would fail to hook the bass securely. I don't know if this is a valid concern, but I can't get it out of my mind.

Dry Flies

Many anglers feel that fishing dry flies for smallmouth bass is the most enjoyable way to take them. I must admit that I'm one of these anglers, I believe this is because each year I find different situations where slightly different dry-fly tactics are much more effective than I had previously realized they would be. This prompts ones expectations and heightens the gratifications of catching the smallmouth bass on dry flies.

Caddisflies

Each spring I look forward to the swarms of natural caddisflies that fly upstream just several feet over the river's surface at dusk. There will often be a mix of emerging flies and those coming back to the stream to deposit their eggs. These busy insects buzzing and drifting along the surface of the stream prompt many bass to rise to intercept them.

The natural caddisfly is one of the first insects on many smallmouth rivers and these dense hatches often bring dozens of bass to the surface in each run.

The gentle runs where the riffles empty into the pools hold many bass at this time and a good tactic is to watch for bass rising to the natural insects and then fish to each fish individually. If you do not see fish feeding on the surface you can still take some nice bass on Elk Hair Caddis and Caddis Buck Dry flies by simply covering the water carefully below these riffles.

In order to fish these runs I use the same tactics whether I'm fishing to specific rising bass or simply covering the water. I set myself up at a forty-five-degree angle about forty feet upstream of the area I plan to fish. I cast just upstream of this anticipated hot spot and let my dry caddisfly drift naturally for several feet then impart a slow twitching action to it by stripping in about two inches of line every five seconds. This causes my fly to act like the real insect and often triggers strikes that I don't get with a naturally drifting dry fly. I wade downstream slowly, methodically covering all of the rising bass and any locations that look like they might hold bass.

Some years when the rivers are low and clear during the caddisfly hatches I've found a different tactic to be more effective than the twitching method. In these conditions the gentle currents encourage the bass to locate on specific feeding stations in the long, flat pools running two to four feet deep where they are now wary and much more selective in their feeding habits. I use an upstream approach under these conditions because it helps me keep from scaring these bass. I like to pick out individual bass and cast an Elk Hair Caddis size 12 several feet above it and let it drift naturally to the bass. This is an exceptionally exciting way to start your dry-fly fishing for the season, and if you don't get nervous standing there with a dozen smallmouths rising within casting distance you'll be one of the few anglers who doesn't.

Early Mayflies

Shortly after the caddisfly hatches are over, and sometimes even overlapping them, some rivers have good mayfly hatches. Several different species can be seen depending upon the specific river, and many anglers refer to most of these as March browns and brown drakes. One can see the duns emerging from the streams from mid-afternoon until dusk. If the hatch is heavy many bass will pull out on feeding stations along the foam lines on the sides of the heavy runs and in front of and beside boulders to sip them in. I like to watch for these surface feeders and go one-on-one with them with an Irresistible or March Brown Dry Fly size 12 fishing upstream just as I would on a trout stream.

I find the most exciting time for fishing the early season mayfly hatches is the last hour of daylight. At this time the spinners return to the stream to mate and deposit their eggs in the stream after which they fall spent onto the surface of the rivers. Their fully extended wings reaching far out from the sides of their bodies and their sometimes present death flutter attract great numbers of bass to feed on the surface. This action is at its best in the upper flats of the main pools because the riffles upstream funnel the flies to the waiting bass.

There are two successful ways to fish this mayfly spinner fall, both of which present a one-on-one challenge with each feeding bass thus putting a demand on the angler's skill. As you'll quickly discover, the slow currents in these flat pools do not carry the spent flies to the bass as fast as they want them so the bass cruise along just beneath the surface and sip in as many as they can.

Mayfly hatches can be very thick on some smallmouth rivers prompting many fish to feed on the surface along the foam lines and around boulders.

The first method calls for watching the rise forms of a specific bass as it cruises from one natural fly to the next to sip them in. Once you see the direction of his path you cast your fly out in front of where you suspect it's headed. You can either allow it to remain motionless on the water and hope it'll come to it or give it a slight twitch to attract its attention—I find the latter ploy works best for me.

A second tactic, that I call "hitting him on the head," is another way to fish for these cruising surface feeders. Here I watch closely and when I see a bass rise to take a spent mayfly I instantly cast my dry fly to the exact spot where it came up. My justification for this "quick draw" technique is that at least for that moment I know precisely where the bass is. Actually, this is a highly effective method, I suspect, because the bass assumes it can get another easy meal without going in search of it.

Damselflies and Dragonflies

Many natural damselflies and dragonflies start showing up over smallmouth rivers in June and continue to increase in number until fall.

Smallmouth bass are show-offs when they attempt to feed on adult damselflies and dragonflies because they leap into the air and grab them as they fly low over the stream. Very few of these natural insects ever land on the stream and drift along the surface, so the bass do not get a shot at them in this form.

Seeing this, I finally realized that the bass's strike is triggered by the *action* of the natural flies as they buzz just above the surface of the stream. From early July until fall those bass you see leaping into the air over the stream are actually after these flies. The dragonflies are such powerful flyers that bass catch few of them, however, they catch great numbers of the damselflies. I've landed many smallmouths that were so stuffed with adult damselflies the backs of their throats were covered with them.

These airborne smallmouths have been presenting such challenging targets to me on the rivers that I fish regularly that I've put an extra effort in refining tactics and fly patterns that will take them. I quickly learned that the actions of my flies, more than their appearances, were what brought the most strikes from the largest bass. Thus I strived to mimic the action of the naturals as they buzzed across the water.

The best flies I've found that helped me duplicate the action of these natural insects are those I've come to refer to as Smallmouth Skaters. These are heavily hackled, palmered long-shank dry flies with outrigger wings tied with buoyant materials. We tie these in blue to match the color of many of the damselflies, olive

At dusk you can catch many nice bass that cruise just below the surface of the rivers to feed on spent mayflies. Watch for their rise form then "hit them on the head".

to match the dragonflies and a brown-grizzly pattern we call the Mr. Rapidan Bass Skater which is highly effective in general use. In use, I dress these liberally with silicone cream, and I dress the whole leader.

The tactic that I like to use with these skaters is to cast them down and across stream at a forty-five-degree angle to the best-looking water or where I've seen a bass leap into the air. Instantly I remove all of the slack with my line hand and extend the rod up and out over the river at a forty-five-degree angle. Using a stiff-arm motion, I quickly get the fly up on its toes and skate it up and across stream in two-foot bursts every five seconds. This lively skating fly motion is often more than the bass can resist and they come racing to the surface to grab the fly. Many of them hit it solidly, but some are poor shots and miss it completely. When this happens, experience has shown me that if I wait about thirty seconds then skate my dry slightly slower over that same spot I can usually take that bass.

If you have never tried skating tactics but would like to have a great amount of fun with it and learn it quickly while taking many nice bass, let me show you the time and place to start.

Go to the river the last hour of daylight in late July or August because there will be great numbers of natural damselflies over the river. Select the tail of a pool where a ledge with a vertical upstream face momentarily slows the current before it spills out over it. Ideally the water immediately upstream of the ledge should be three to four feet deep. Cautiously wade into the river forty feet upstream of the ledge. Cast across and down stream at a forty-five-degree angle so your Skater falls about five feet upstream of the ledge. Instantly begin the skating motion described earlier so your big dry fly bounces along the surface of the river right in

Natural dragonflies and damselflies are present in great numbers on smallmouth rivers all summer where their low-flying antics prompt the bass to leap from the stream to grab them.

front of the ledge. Slowly wade all the way across the river using this tactic so every bass holding in front of that ledge gets a look at your fly.

This is highly effective because you have taken advantage of the two basic requirements for successful smallmouth fly-fishing. That is, you are fishing your flies over ideal feeding stations and making them act like the natural foods bass are accustomed to feeding on in that area.

These three Smallmouth Skaters are a great joy to fish and will take many bass as you dance them gently along the surface of the rivers. Left to right: Murray's Olive Dragonfly Skater, Mr. Rapidan Skater and Murray's Blue Damsel Skater.

I've had great success with Smallmouth Skaters using a slightly different tactic during those years when the rivers get extremely low late in the summer. Under these conditions the large smallmouths often do not come out to feed until the last half hour of daylight. The tails of the freestone pools where the water is two to three feet deep over a cobblestone bottom as it funnels out of the pool above are ideal feeding areas at this time. On many rivers, these tails may range from one hundred to two hundred feet wide and it often seems like the bass spread out across them like a military formation on drill field. These bass are quite bold in the fading light and quickly grab any natural food that drifts by.

When I fish these pool tails with a Smallmouth Skater I enter the river at the riffle below them and turn to wade gently upstream just far enough to allow me to be in complete control of my fly as I cast it upstream onto the flat water in the pool upstream—I don't want the fast water to grab my line and drag the fly out of the pool. As soon as the Skater lands on the water I remove the slack and with my fly rod high in the air I dance it across the surface in two six-inch bursts, then let it rest. Often this is all it takes to get a solid strike...remember these bass are now here to feed and they don't want to miss anything that looks good to eat.

This tactic is so effective that I've often seen the wake of a bass coming from ten feet away to take my fly. And I can assure you when this happens about every third or fourth cast you'll get so excited that you'll forget all of your well-developed angling axioms. It really is tough to know exactly when to strike in this low light level as you watch the bass's wake. If you hit too soon you'll take it away from the bass. If you delay your strike for too long it'll eject the fly and you miss it—you have to time your strike perfectly. This can be so exciting, but unnerving, it's probably good that it lasts only a half hour each evening.

Some areas that produce well with Skaters throughout the day include the three- to four-foot-deep cuts between river crossing ledges, around aquatic grassbeds and around brush piles.

Smallmouths feed aggressively each evening and you can often see their wakes coming a gre
and punching out long casts.

distance as they move in to take your Skaters. You can get great fishing by wading cautiously

Usually one's greatest success in taking bass feeding on damselflies is dependent upon fishing your flies in a manner that mimics the action of the real insects. For me this means I want to keep my flies skating.

Grasshoppers

Late in the summer, natural grasshoppers are large enough to be attractive to bass.

Smallmouth rivers which flow beside pasture fields and hay fields often carry many grasshoppers to smallmouths that hold close to the banks. I've seen late-summer thunderstorms with strong winds blow great numbers of grasshoppers into the rivers where the bank-side currents act like conveyer belts as they deliver the helpless grasshoppers to the bass. When this happens you might have more than a dozen bass feeding along a hundred feet of the bank.

Even if I do not see feeding bass I often get great action by fishing flies such as Dave's Hoppers sizes 8 and 10 and Shenk's Hopper size 10 along these banks.

Natural grasshoppers kicking along the surface of the river often bring splashy, water-throwing rises from bass as they race to grab them.

I use two different tactics here depending upon the stream level.

If there is a good stream level and the water is three to four feet deep along these banks I like to wade down the river about forty feet out from the bank. I cast my hopper down and across stream at about a ten-degree angle so it falls close to the bank. A gentle strip-pause-strip retrieve that imitates the kicking action of a struggling grasshopper usually catches more bass than a quiet drifting action. Eventually the force of the current on the line and leader pulls the fly away from the bank and produces an unnatural action on the fly. When this happens I wade five feet down the river and cast my hopper back against the bank and repeat the strip-pause-strip retrieve.

Late in the summer David Foster caught many bass by imparting a kicking action to a grasshopper dry fly as you drift it along the banks and ledges.

If the rivers are very low and clear and the water along these pasture field banks is less than three feet deep, I usually use an upstream approach to fish my hoppers so I don't scare the bass with my approach. I get about ten feet out from the bank and cast my hoppers up and across stream so they land close to the bank about forty feet upstream. I use a slow line-hand twitching action to make my fly kick gently down the river, just like a real grasshopper.

This is a very effective tactic for smallmouth and even though it is quite similar to trout tactics on the large river I recommend not going finer than a 3X leader for bass. The large hoppers can easily twist finer tippets and weaken them to the point that you can easily break off a big bass when you set the hook.

Late-Season Mayflies

The white Miller *(Ephoron leukon)* mayfly hatch begins from the middle to the latter part of the summer depending upon the latitude of the stream. This is a very heavy hatch on many rivers with the peak of the concentration lasting about two weeks. However, when the stream conditions are ideal you may get four to five weeks of great dry-fly fishing when these flies are on the water.

The duns start emerging about an hour before dark. The molting, mating, egg laying and spinner fall take place as darkness approaches and may continue after dark. With this is mind, you want to plan your evening's fishing carefully. For example, I select flies that will float well even after I've caught many fish on them, I have a good flashlight handy in my vest in case I break a fly off and need to replace it, I plan the area to fish so I don't hook trees on my back cast in the dark,

I plan the precise spot I intend to wade out of the stream in order to miss steep banks, poison ivy and barbed wire fences.

My favorite standard dry flies for this hatch are the Light Humpy size 12 and Irresistible size 10. These are durable flies constructed with elk hair and deer hair that keep them floating well even after catching many bass. This is a great help because you don't have to constantly change flies in the fading light. Many experienced anglers devise their own flies for this hatch which are very effective. For instance, Bob Abraham, a master of this hatch on the Potomac River, has developed a great pattern using a white dubbed body with a white deer-hair head.

As the hatch begins each day, a standard upstream dry-fly presentation is very effective. When you spot a rise, pause and wait a few minutes to see if it comes up at the same spot again. If it does you can assume the bass is on a feeding station and you can cast your dry fly two feet upstream of the bass and let it drift naturally to it. Many of these bass will take your fly solidly.

When dusk approaches you will have both duns hatching and spinners coming back to deposit their eggs. This profusion of flies on the surface of the river brings a great number of bass to the surface and they feed in what can best be described as a frenzy. It is not at all unusual to have over two dozen bass feeding on the surface within casting distance.

This wild display of so many feeding fish and the fast-approaching darkness prompts one to feel rushed in an attempt to catch every fish he can while he can still see what's happening. In order to give myself a slight edge under these conditions I try to position myself so I'm fishing into the west. Even though the sun is below the horizon there is enough light reflecting off the surface of the water to enable me to squeeze in an extra fifteen to twenty minutes of great dry-fly fishing. A second ploy I use at this time is to twitch my dry fly along the surface about two inches every five seconds. With all of the natural mayflies on the surface I believe this slight movement of my dry fly helps get a bass's attention and prompts it to take this rather than the naturals.

Every smallmouth angler should fish a good white Miller hatch at least once just to see the abundance of mayflies on the river and the bass gorging themselves on them.

Hexagenia Mayflies

The *Hexagenia* is on many smallmouth rivers in August and although this hatch is not as heavy as the white Miller, the size of this fly often brings some of the largest bass to the surface.

The tactics I use to fish this hatch for smallmouths are much like some of the trout tactics I use on the large rivers in the Rockies. By late summer, when these flies hatch on smallmouth rivers, the water levels are often low and the large bass

The author enjoys fishing the *Hexagenia* hatch because many large bass come to the surface to feed on the naturals and take his flies readily.

are quite wary. A cautious upstream approach helps me get within casting distance of many bass that I'm sure I would scare if I waded downstream.

As dusk approaches I look for rise forms where the main currents brush against the aquatic grassbeds in water about hip deep. If I spot a riser I cast an Irresistible size 8 dry fly about two feet upstream of the feeding bass and let the current deliver it naturally to the bass. Most of these bass take the dry as soon as it drifts into their feeding station. If I do not see a rise form within casting distance as I wade upstream I cast my dry fly upstream above each point where the current will drift it along the undercut edges of the grassbeds. Often the bass will be holding here just waiting for some food to drift by and they will take my dry fly as soon as they see it.

As you can see, there is good dry-fly fishing for smallmouth from spring until fall and by adapting your tactics and flies to the specific conditions you can get great action.

Chapter 8

Floating A Smallmouth River

Floating smallmouth rivers in a canoe, drift boat or kick boat can open many doors for you.When the rivers are too high to wade comfortably and safely you can often get outstanding fishing by drifting along and fishing the banks and ledge outcroppings. If there are remote stretches of a river with limited road access you can easily float into these areas and find great fishing where the bass receive only light angling pressure.

In some parts of the country, where rivers flow through low-gradient terrain, the riffles and rocky portions of the rivers, which are the preferred habitat of the smallmouths may be widely separated up and down the river by miles of slow,

One of the most rewarding aspects of floating a smallmouth river in a drift boat or canoe is being able to share the experience with a good friend. A large fish, a well-presented bug or just simply the appreciation of the country you're drifting through is magnified as it is shared.

sand-bottom stretches that hold mostly sunfish. After you've caught your fill of sunfish and properly inflated your ego you can drift on downstream to the next stretch of ideal smallmouth cover.

One of the most rewarding aspects of floating a smallmouth river in a drift boat or canoe is being able to share the experience with a good friend. A large fish, a well-presented bug or just simply the appreciation of the country you're drifting through is magnified as it is shared.

The logistics of a float trip are pretty simple, but here are some things we've learned on our guide trips over the years. Spot the boat-carrying rig at the lower end of the float so if you float until dark you don't have to shuttle cars when you can't see well and are worn out. This is also advantageous if you hit a bad storm late in the day and want to drift out and finish early.

When I'm drifting, I always like to carry a personal floatation device for each person in the boat (this is the law in some state) as well as a raincoat for each person. Drinks (non alcoholic) and food are essential on a long float trip.

Before you leave on your float trip check the stream level on the USGS website that shows "real time stream flows", then check the clarity of the river when you arrive at the launch point. In some cases the water level is fine, but recent rains over cultivated fields can cause the river to be too discolored for good fishing.

Good topo maps are helpful if you plan to float new stretches of a river. Never float through water that looks too heavy to be safe. Once, in Labrador, our guides wisely had us walk a hundred yards around some powerful white water which they shot in canoes and then picked us up downstream. If you drift into a sharp turn on a river that looks a little heavy you can almost always find the slowest water on the inside of the turn. If you're concerned that any stretch of water is too difficult to float safely, rope your boat through it as you wade downstream in the calm water. Also, on sharp turns be on the lookout for fallen tree "sweepers" that might block your way.

Angling Tactics For Float Trips

An exceptionally effective tactic when floating a smallmouth river is to fish along the bank carefully as you drift downstream.

Your most consistent success will come by properly evaluating the banks as you drift along. Those streches that provide food, cover and shade will give you the best action with the largest bass. If the water along the bank is three to four feet deep over a cobblestone bottom you'll have such food as hellgrammites and chub minnows along with any food items that fall into the river such as mice, frogs and grasshoppers. This depth provides good cover for the bass and if the bank is undercut or there are logs or downfalls these provide great appeal for the largest bass. Shade from large trees along the bank, especially those with limbs out over the river, is a big plus for smallmouths. Basically, I like to fish the east banks in the

A kick boat is a good craft for float trips for smallmouth bass because it is light enough to put in and take out at any point and it can be easily maneuvered to fish all types of cover.

mornings and the west banks in the evenings to take advantage of the shade. Aquatic grassbeds in water over three feet deep along the banks should be fished very thoroughly.

Conversely, don't waste much time along banks where the stream bottom is sandy, muddy or solid ledges or if the water is only a foot deep.

It is important to drift off the bank at a distance that will give you good control of the fly placement while not scaring the fish with the craft. About forty to fifty feet is right in most cases.

If you are using a canoe you will get your best control if the person in the back does the paddling while the person in the front does the fishing. In a drift boat, one person rows while the person in the front and the person in the back concentrate on fishing. At periodic intervals you can rotate around in these crafts so everyone gets time to fish. A kick boat that allows you to control it with both oars and flippers is ideal for fishing the banks. You can kick with your flippers to keep the proper distance off the bank as you drift along and position the boat at the perfect angle to allow you to make a perfect presentation.

Surface fishing with hard-head bugs, deer-hair bugs and big dry flies is very popular when floating the rivers. On our guide trips we've discovered that many anglers are most effective with these surface patterns if they cast downstream at a ten- to twenty-degree angle ahead of the boat to drop the bug as close to the bank as possible. In many cases the bug is drifting at the same speed as the boat and a slight stripping action with the line hand is all that's needed to get a strike. If the current starts pulling on the line causing the bug to drag away from the bank too quickly, a simple upstream mend is all that's needed to continue a natural bug action. Depending on the speed of the currents between the boat and the bank you may be able to get a realistic drift of your bug for fifteen feet, but when your bug gets back even with the boat or the current pulls it so far off the bank that you are not getting strikes, pick it up and cast it out ahead of the boat again.

A slightly different twist to this tactic is to add a dropper fly on about two feet of 3X tippet off the bend of the hook of a popper with an improved clinch knot. On a hard-head bug size 4 or 6 a fly such as a size 10 Pearl Marauder Streamer is ideal—larger streamers than this can sink the bug. Fish this two-fly rig the same way you would if you were fishing just the bug and watch for the strike on the bug.

When you are drifting the banks and fishing an underwater single-fly rig with any streamer or nymph it is best to cast straight in toward the bank. Drop your fly as close to the bank as you can get it, and be ready for the strike at any moment. Bass are holding here to feed and they often take the fly within the first several seconds. As you are drifting along be sure to remove all of the slack line with your line hand so you are tight on the fly and can easily detect the strike.

Riffles provide great smallmouth fishing and can be effectively fished in several different ways when floating a river. The easiest way to thoroughly fish a riffle when floating the river is to beach your craft at the upper end, get out and wade and fish the whole area carefully. When you are finished you can wade back up to your craft and float on down to the next area you want to fish.

Another effective way to fish the riffles is to float down the side of them and anchor just below the spot where the riffles empty into the main part of the pools. From this position you can cast across stream with nymphs and streamers and fish these back across the interface where the bass hold in the pools to feed on any food washing out of the riffles. After thoroughly covering all of the water within reach you can lift the anchor just slightly and drift downstream about twenty feet, anchor solidly again and fish this area thoroughly.

Fishing the riffles is easy in a continuous-tube oval-shaped kick boat because you can just stand up on the bottom of the river when you come to good-looking water and fish it completely, then slowly wade on downstream to cover the whole area. The kick boat is so buoyant that it just rests lightly on the surface and does not interfere with your fishing.

When I started testing various kick boats to select the ones I wanted to sell in my fly shop I was pleasantly surprised by how I was able to drift into flat, spooky water and catch bass that I had been scaring even when wading as carefully as I could. It was late August and my rivers were unusually low and the sections I fished regularly were reduced to twenty- to forty-foot-wide strips of open water meandering between thick beds of aquatic grass. I found that by using my foot flippers I could drift quietly to within casting distance of many large bass and catch them in the open channels between the grassbeds and open bays within the grassbeds.

The distance of a float trip is a matter of personal preference. Personally, I don't like to float more than five miles because I like to stop along the way and wade to fish some of the riffles and grassbeds.

Chapter 9

Fishing for Smallmouths in Ponds and Lakes

Many anglers are much more familiar with fly-fishing for smallmouth in rivers than they are in lakes and ponds. One can definitely draw on this knowledge to help locate the best area to fish in these large bodies of water.

Smallmouth are definitely attracted to those areas in lakes that have rocky bottoms. Sunken islands, shoals, rocky drop-offs along the banks, man-made reefs and the mouths of feeder streams all provide what the smallmouth like. Not only do these areas provide the ideal cover bass want, but many of their foods such as nymphs, minnows and crawfish are found here.

I especially like to fish the rocky areas along the bank where trees and shrubs give shade over the edge of the lake. Logs and downfalls in the water not only provide ideal shade for bass, but the security the overhead cover affords will often attract the largest bass.

Kick boats are ideal for fishing lakes because you can move quietly along the shore and cover the best water without scaring the bass.

Aquatic grassbeds usually hold many large bass that move into these areas to feed on the minnows and nymphs. When you find these grassbeds at the mouths of feeder streams that enter your lake, give them extra attention because the cool water of the stream often pulls the bass like a magnet and the slight chemical change can boost the growth of food.

My favorite tactic in lakes and ponds is to fish the shore edges with surface bugs. A broad variety of bugs work here but I get my best results with a gray or chartreuse Chuggar. I cast the bug within a foot or two of the bank and let it lie motionless for about thirty seconds. Often the strike will come at this time so be ready to set the hook quickly. In many clear lakes you will see the bass coming up to take the bug and in others you may see its wake as it heads for your bug. In both of these cases it takes self-control to keep from setting the hook too soon and taking the bug away from the bass. If I don't get a strike at this point I impart two line-hand strips of about six inches to the bug then allow it to remain still for about a minute then apply two more strips. I use this strip-pause-strip method to fish the bug out about ten feet then pick it up and cast it to a new spot about five feet further along the bank while moving the boat or canoe along slowly.

If the surface game doesn't work, my next ploy is to go to underwater flies.

I choose streamers and nymphs that match the natural foods the bass are accustomed to feeding on in lakes. Shiners, shad-like minnows, dragonfly nymphs, damselfly nymphs and crawfish are all important food items on various lakes. Some of my most productive flies include Olive Strymphs, Dragonfly Nymphs, Clouser Crawfish, Silver Outcast Streamer, Pearl Marauder, Shenk's

John Coleman's expression captures the deep gratification one derives from smallmouth angling, showing that "before God and fish all are equal".

White Streamer, Murray's Wounded Shiner, and Clouser Deep Silver Shiner all in sizes 4, 6, and 8.

Some of the most exciting fishing in lakes takes place early in the mornings and late in the evenings when the bass prowl the aquatic grassbeds to feed on the minnows that live there. If you see the minnows splashing across the surface, cast your fly out in front of the minnows and impart a fast stripping action to attract a bass's attention. Even after the minnow stops scurrying across the surface, it is wise to methodically cast your flies throughout the area because the bass is usually close by. Even if you don't see an active "chase" you can still catch many bass around grassbeds by fishing them thoroughly with surface bugs, streamers and nymphs. In most cases I like to use floating lines around aquatic grassbeds.

Rocky shorelines are also very productive at dusk and dawn. I usually try a floating line here first, but if I don't catch as many bass as I think I should I switch to a sink-tip fly line in which the first twelve to fifteen feet sinks at 2.5 to 4.25 inches per second and use a five-foot leader. I cast a streamer in tight against the shore and allow it to sink, then use my line hand to impart two slow, four-inch strips to crawl the fly across the bottom. I pause to allow the sink-tip of the line to pull the fly down to the bottom, then strip it again. I continue this strip-sink-strip action as I fish the streamer out away from the shore. Since most lakes get deeper further out from the banks you need to pause longer between strips so the sink-tip of the line will pull the fly down.

If you are fishing a shoreline that gets deep real quickly, or sunken islands or around boulders in water over fifteen feet deep, you might get your best results by using a sinking head fly line in which the first twenty-five to thirty feet of the line sinks at about five to six inches per second.

The tactics for fishing deeply with these sinking-head rigs are much the same as with the shorter sink-tip lines except that now a jigging action can also be very effective. In order to impart this jigging-crawling action to your nymphs and streamers allow the fly line to pull the fly to the bottom on the presentation cast, then use your arm to slowly lift the whole rod straight up about two feet while holding the line firmly in your line hand. Slowly drop the rod back down while simultaneously stripping in about a foot of slack line with your line hand. Continue this lifting and diving motion all the way back to the boat, then pick it up and cast it to a new location about five feet to the side of the previous cast and repeat the retrieve. This method enables you to fish your fly within view of every bass before you. After you've covered a comfortable arc before you, move the boat along slowly and repeat the sequence.

When fishing deeply you should strive to be very alert to the slightest bump, tap or line movement that can signal a bass's take. Don't ever assume that unusual

Sunken islands and large boulders a short distance from the banks can give you great action by fishing your nymphs and streamers slowly along the lake bottom.

bump was your fly hitting a boulder. Set the hook firmly because it just might have been the largest bass in the lake.

The basic part of the strike on deeply sunken flies is a firm uplifting motion of the rod arm which lifts the whole rod. This puts the butt of the rod into the strike which helps telegraph the strike deeply. Simultaneously with the rod strike, it is very helpful to impart a solid jerk with your line hand which strips the line in about three feet. In many cases this combination of a firm rod lift and fast line-hand stripping strike will enable you to hook many bass that you would have missed otherwise.

Fishing for smallmouth bass in lakes and ponds can provide some of the most gratifying rewards of this fine game. Since many large bass are found here the exciting expectations of taking these big fish are always on one's mind. Also, a large amount of the time fishing these large bodies of water is spent fishing with surface bugs and the thrill of action played out right in front of you in clear view definitely adds great excitement to this angling game.

Index

Fishing the shaded river banks with surface bugs as you drift along in a boat is a great way to catch big bass.

GREAT BOOKS FOR BASS FISHING

HOT BASS FLIES: PATTERNS & TACTICS FROM THE EXPERTS

Deke Meyer

Fly-fishing for bass is hotter than ever, and so are the bass flies used to catch them. Combining traditional fur and feathers with modern synthetics, innovative designers have developed bass flies that wiggle and waggle, spin and dart, pop and gurgle, slink and undulate, all of which drive bass wild. In *Hot Bass Flies*, Deke Meyer shares over 200 exceptional bass flies from experts known and unknown alike. 8 1/2 x 11 inches, 136 pages, full-color.

SB: $24.95 **ISBN: 1-57188-285-5**
UPC: 0-81127-00103-3

Spiral HB: $39.95 **ISBN: 1-57188-286-3**
UPC: 0-81127-00104-0

LARGEMOUTH BASS FLY-FISHING BEYOND THE BASICS

Terry and Roxanne Wilson

Largemouth bass are capable of jerking the rod from your hands if you're unprepared for the strike. In this book, the Wilsons discuss: understanding bass habitat; approach, delivery, and fly animation; fishing the shallows; the vertical drop; fishing the mid-depths; going deep; time, weather, and locational patterns; plus seasonal and night fishing information; fly patterns; and more. This book will show you how to catch more of these fast, powerful, acrobatic fish. 6 x 9 inches, 160 pages.

SB: $16.00 **ISBN: 1-57188-215-4**
UPC: 0-66066-00429-1

FIT TO FISH

Stephen L. Hisey, P.T,
Keith R. Berend, M.D.

Survey all your fishing buddies and you'll find that the vast majority of them suffer from some kind of shoulder, elbow, or wrist pain due to casting all day long. *Fit to Fish* explains the causes, and describes treatment and prevention techniques utilizing conditioning, stretching, and exercise, and also includes many photographs that greatly enhance this text. Berend, a surgeon, and Hisey, a physical therapist, have 75 years of combined experience treating the human body. Topics covered include: Pain and its origins; self treatment; shoulder impingement syndrome; tendonitis and Carpal Tunnel; low back pain; knee and ankle pain and instability; glossary; and more. 6 x 9 inches, 160 pages.

SB: $19.95 **ISBN: 1-57188-354-1**
UPC: 0-81127-00188-0

WHAT FISH SEE

Dr. Colin Kageyama, O.D.

An in-depth examination by Dr. Colin Kageyama of how and what fish see. This important book will help all anglers to design better flies and lures by its explanation of the physical processes of light in water and consequently how colors change and are perceived by fish in varying conditions of depth, turbidity, and light. Excellent illustrations by Vic Erickson and color plates that show startling color changes. This book will change the way you fish! 6 x 9 inches, 184 pages.

SB: $19.95 **ISBN: 1-57188-140-9**
UPC: 0-66066-00340-9

BLUEGILL FLY FISHING & FLIES

Roxanne and Terry Wilson

A bluegill's yanking, diving, twisting battles make for a tenacious opponent, especially on ultralight equipment. The Wilsons share: proper equipment; best flies, including their recipes and techniques for using them; identifying productive bluegill waters; bluegill habits and behaviors; effective presentations; and many more tips learned over their combined 75 years of experience fishing for bluegill. 6 x 9 inches, 151 pages.

SB: $16.95 **ISBN: 1-57188-176-X**
UPC: 0-66066-00378-2

PLANK COOKING: THE ESSENCE OF NATURAL WOOD

By Scott & Tiffany Haugen

In *Plank Cooking: The Essence of Natural Wood*, globe-trotting authors, Scott & Tiffany Haugen, share some of the world's most exquisite flavors. Thai red curry prawns, Achiote pork roast, pesto couscous stuffed chicken, and caramelized bananas are just a few of the unique recipes brought to life in this fully illustrated, one-of-a-kind book.

In the oven or on a grill, plank cooking is fun and simple. This book outlines how to master the art of plank cooking, from seasoning planks to detailed cooking tips in over 100 easy-to-follow recipes. Though exotic tastes prevail, the ingredients used in *Plank Cooking* are easy to find in most grocery stores. Full color; 6 x 9; 152 pages

Spiral SB: $19.95 **ISBN: 1-57188-332-0**
UPC: 0-81127-00164-4